Selling
Securities
Successfully

SELLING

SECURITIES

SUCCESSFULLY

Leo Y. Fleur

Prentice-Hall, Inc.

Englewood Cliffs, N. J.

Fifth printing....... May, 1969

PRINTED IN THE UNITED STATES OF AMERICA

80597—B&P

To CHARLES E. BACON, my first and best teacher

FOREWORD

SELLING SECURITIES SUCCESSFULLY IS AN ART RE-
quiring the highest ethical standards, extensive
product knowledge, and much hard work.

"Requiring the highest ethical standards"—
because the customer's interest must come first.
The successful securities salesman knows his
customer and helps him achieve his financial objectives.

"Requiring extensive product knowledge"—because the more knowledgeable the
registered representative is about securities and
market procedures, the better the service he is
able to render. *No one* knows the future of "the
market" or of any particular security. It is a
human impossibility for any registered representative to be 100% right in all his recommendations. The good "R.R.," using his better product knowledge, keeps his average high and cor-
rects errors as they become evident.

"Requiring much hard work"—because it is a fact of life that a registered representative must sell in order to earn his livelihood. First, he must attract customers, and then he must keep them. Neither is easy to do, and each requires sales ability and effort.

Keeping the best interest of each customer in mind, the registered representative must "write tickets" to avoid starving to death. There is no secret that his earnings are based on the commissions he generates. It is a compliment to the overwhelming majority of the tens of thousands of securities salesmen, and to the regulatory agencies, both voluntary and governmental, that the selling standards and practices in the industry are so high.

Those in the business, and presumably most of those in the investing public, know that the registered representative's income is based on the orders he processes. However, within the business there apparently has been some reluctance to face up to the fact that successful securities salesmanship requires successful *selling*. Certainly, there is little that has been published on this subject.

This book does not skirt the issue. It is about how to *sell securities*. Ethical selling is the basic assumption throughout. The author, based upon his years of successful experience, sets forth in clear and understandable language workable day-to-day, week-to-week, and month-to-month procedures a registered representative can follow to become a successful securities salesman. He offers no "gimmicks," only suggestions which require hard work to implement. They are proven, practical and helpful.

To the writer's knowledge, *Selling Securities Success-*

fully, of all publications on selling, is the first full-length book devoted exclusively to the selling of securities. It meets a long-felt need.

DAVID E. BUNTING
President, New York Institute of Finance

CONTENTS

[xi]

Chapter	Page

Selling
Securities
Successfully

CHAPTER 1

ORGANIZING YOUR TIME

Which Man Are You?

Either you have passed the qualifying examinations recently and are a newly registered representative, or you have been in the business for some time but haven't done well. Your firm has given you an executive's swivel chair, a handsome desk, and all the paraphernalia you need in order to do business. Quite appropriately, a large stack of empty order tickets sits in the middle of your desk, and your livelihood depends on how many tickets you will be able to fill out. Well, what do you do now?

You can be one of those men who comes into the office each day without knowing what he will do. Before him on the desk are scattered prospect cards, newspaper leads, and some names, and as if by whim, he selects a name to call. After calling two or three names, he finds some other activity, usually non-productive, such as watching the tape or talking to his neighbor. Although such a man may have the desire to work, he has not disciplined himself into a fixed *pattern* of work.

You must be the man who has planned his efforts and knows what to do and how to do it.

Analyze Your Job

Your job can be broken down into five major categories, and you must organize your time into compartments so that there will be enough for each of these essential activities:

1. Soliciting New Business
2. Servicing Existing Accounts
3. Reading and Studying Financial Reports
4. Keeping Records of Accounts and Prospects
5. Community Work

The question now arises as to how much time should be given to each activity. The newly registered representative should unquestionably spend the greater portion of his time soliciting new accounts.

Tell Your Story

All your other activities must be subordinated to that of speaking to people. You will need to find every means possible to present your product to people. You will have to allot time during market hours, in the evening, and on

Saturday for this activity. The importance of constantly speaking to people cannot be overemphasized, for this is the only way that customers can be made. How, when, and where to make your contacts is discussed in a later chapter.

The importance of speaking to people was realized by S.K., who today is a partner in a small member firm. He entered the business six years ago with four modest accounts. S.K. spent his working day on the phone, finding every excuse or reason to call people. Most of these people did not become customers. But many did, enough to give him a sizeable sales production.

Once accounts are acquired, they can readily be serviced during market hours. This service will consist mainly of answering calls for last quotes, sales, and current statistical information.

In speaking to your accounts, confine the conversation to the business at hand and do not waste time in unnecessary conversation. Talking to existing accounts takes precedence over talking to prospective accounts, but one does not converse just for the sake of talking. The party at the other end of the line will have more respect for you if your conversation is concise, accurate, and factual.

Find Suitable Stories to Tell

The reading of newspapers and financial and statistical reports should be done only at those times when you cannot talk to people. If you commute, your trip affords an excellent opportunity to keep up on this reading. A most effective time to study is just prior to going to sleep, for you will be more relaxed and better able to retain the technical material.

Your purpose in reading and studying is to provide yourself with material to present to your prospects and accounts. If you have been out of school for a while, retention of study material may prove a little difficult. But one's memory can be trained, and by assiduous study the material will be retained. As you continue in your study habits, retention will become better. Having set times for reading makes the study process easier. In an era of enlightened customers, only the registered representative who commits himself to continual study will be able to talk intelligently to the public. Customers who have accumulated enough money to invest generally have the ability to weigh accurately facts and possibilities. You will have to know your material, and, just as important, know how to communicate it to your clientele.

Part of your study time may have to be devoted to improving your ability to communicate. You may need practice in diction, voice inflection, or in building a larger vocabulary. Take the necessary time to improve yourself in these areas, for effective communications will make your job much easier.

Plan Your Daily Work

Saturday morning should be used to organize your work for the coming week. Make out a schedule of calls for each day of the week. Leave time for calls which cannot be planned in advance. Each evening of the week you should review your Saturday Master Plan, adding the calls which arose as a result of that day's work. For example, while making your calls on Monday, you may have been referred to someone whom you could reach on Wednesday. This person should now be added to your list of Wednesday calls.

The successful salesman is the one who has scheduled his work. Each morning that he comes into the office, he knows what he will do that day. He has prepared himself, so that when the unexpected happens, as it often does in the securities business, he can take it in stride. He is like the captain of a ship who, although steering a straight course, can handle any storm which may arise. If you come into the office unprepared for the expected, you will never survive the unexpected occurrences. Being prepared for any situation calls for preplanning and the keeping of records.

On Saturday morning, when you make your plan of activities for the week, list your calls for each day of the week and the reasons for those calls. A typical page may look like this:

Monday

Name	Number	Reason	Comments
John Aster	BA 9-2254	Call Back	
Abner Dunn	GI 7-8456	Growth Stocks	
Gary Haines	FI 6-9999	Call Back	
Ted Fox	TR 5-9424	Mutual Fund	
Dan Egan	HI 9-3425	Referred by Kane	

Lunch with Holt

Ben Garret	TE 8-6598	Call Back
Sam Lewis	PR 9-2451	Call Back—
		coppers
Jack Mayer	TI 4-3286	Cold Call
Arnold Kramp	GE 7-4289	Cold Call

Outside Calls

| Phil Tern | 444 5th Ave. | Interview |

Evening Calls

| Phil Norris | TR 4-9827 | Lead |
| Don Henry | ED 2-9845 | Lead |

And so, for each day of the week you will plan what you will be doing. You will not be one of those men who come into the office each morning with no idea of what he will do that day, and who leaves every activity either to impulse or to chance. By preparing your list in advance you are assuring your success. As you proceed in your work during the week, necessary calls will have to be added to each day's list. A call to Sam Lewis on Monday may lead to a referral to his friend Lou Gaines. You will then add Gaines' name to Tuesday's list of calls.

Although Saturday has been designated for planning the coming week, it may be advantageous to also spend some time making calls. A great many businessmen are in their offices on Saturdays. They are usually less distracted by incoming calls and other mid-week pressures, and will be more easily accessible.

As a case in point, the writer L.F. devoted Saturday mornings to making calls and Saturday afternoons to planning work for the week. The businessman called upon at that time was more relaxed and was easier to deal with. He also enjoyed discussing his finances in a more leisurely atmosphere.

You will notice some cold calls on the above list. Actually your list of cold calls should be considerably larger and may require a complete page of its own. Where you will make a preponderance of cold calls, prepare a page for such calls with these headings:

Name   Business   Phone   Comments   Date

Techniques for making cold calls will appear later in the book.

The registered representative's day would typically proceed in this fashion, with minor alterations:

9:00 A.M.	Arrival in office
9–9:30	Addressing mailing pieces
9:30–10	Calling customers or prospective customers for pre-opening orders
10–10:15	Seeing and analyzing market openings
10:15–12	Calling prospects and/or customers
12–12:30	Lunch
12:30–2	Addressing mailing pieces, and taking calls
2–3:45	Calling suspects, prospects, and customers
3:45–4	Entering records of day's business
4:00–5:00	Two or more cold calls in person
5:00–6:00	Travelling home—studying financial reports
8:00–9:00	Phone calls to prospects
9:00–10:00	Studying reports

As you can see in the above review of a typical day, there is no room for anything but determined work and sustained effort. Unless such a schedule is maintained, the registered representative has little opportunity for success.

Plan Far More Than You Can Accomplish

As you progress in your work, you will find that maintaining a tight schedule is increasingly difficult. As carefully as you may plan, the unforeseen happens every day and throws you off your track. At the end of the day, as you review what you had intended to do, you are perturbed because you could not complete your day's work. *This is good!* The man who completes his plan has not set a heavy enough pace for himself. Also, the fact that we have not completed our plan for the day makes us review our activities in order to determine what we can dispose of, that is, those minor things which we are now doing that take away time from more essential activities.

Study the Habits of the Successful Men Around You

The next time you are in your firm's board room, spend some time observing men who are successful. You are sure to notice that there is no wasted motion about them. Everything they do has a purpose, and is done quietly and efficiently. It is very much like watching a good infielder catch a batted ball and throw it to first—no wasted motion, only economy of movement to attain a definite purpose. He looks neither right nor left, does not consult with anyone else on the field, and makes his throw accurately.

You too must work to achieve this harmony of purpose. You are at that desk alone. Every time you get on the phone you are like that infielder, and every move you make must be made with finesse and accuracy. Every time you

send a piece of mail, it has to be sent for a specific reason—
to achieve a specific purpose. It must be either to interest
a prospect or inform a client. You have just so many hours
in the day to do all these things, and should you spend too
much time on one and neglect the others, your business
will suffer. It will not be an easy job to strike the correct
balance among all your required chores, but it will be a
necessary job.

Your most important task is to talk to as many people
as possible. This activity takes precedence over all others.
Subordinate all your other activities to this one. Remember, it is more important to make cold calls than it is to do
mailing; and it is more important to talk to prospects than
it is to watch the tape.

Toward this purpose, you could also include among
your activities the giving of talks before clubs and groups.
However, do not undertake such lectures unless you are
sufficiently sophisticated in the securities business.

Record Keeping Is a Sign of Good Work Habits

Record keeping is a relatively simple matter if done
every day, and should take no more than half an hour.
Records are necessary to help you service accounts properly. Most records can be entered at the close of the market
from 3:30 to 4:00.

Beware of These Trouble Spots

A review of the day's work may reveal several sore
spots, such as these:

—Spent too much time on the phone with my customer,
Mrs. Hart. She places an order every six months but wants

a daily market report (which she can just as easily get by buying a morning newspaper).

—Took too long on lunch hour. Went out with some of the fellows from the office and decided to have lunch at that swanky new place—it took two hours.

—Addressed and sent out mail to some cold prospects who were just mailed material two weeks ago.

—Analyzed that report on Gare Corp. at my desk instead of at home. Could have made six calls during that time.

—Got into a discussion of the next possible move by the Federal Reserve with K.L. across the aisle. Had a very heated discussion. Neither of us sold any stocks, however.

—Watched the opening until 11:00.

—Started watching the close at 2:00 and didn't finish until 3:40.

—Left at 3:45.

—Forgot to call Mr. Mond. Lost the scrap of paper with his number on it.

—Left my list of prospects at home. Couldn't make any calls.

—Called Mr. Galt four times today and four times yesterday. Will call him again four times tomorrow. He likes to hear about the market. He's a nice old guy. Used to have lots of money.

—Called Dr. Green today. Suggested I call him back. I'll call back next month.

—It was raining today. Couldn't make any cold calls. (What better time to find people in their offices!)

—It was too (choose one) hot__ cold__ damp__ windy__ to make cold calls.

—Had to get off that 300-share order; couldn't talk to anyone else today. It was a good day's business. (But where will tomorrow's business come from?)

It is imperative that you take time out to review your activities in order to be sure that you are not wasting time on unessential matters. There is no room for "extra fat"—your work must be lean and concise.

Today's Order Was Yesterday's Work

If you plan your work and work your plan, each day's business will take care of itself. You may hear a registered representative say, "I don't know where my next order is coming from." If he had planned his work he would not need to worry about where his orders are coming from. They would be coming from the work he did a year ago, six months ago, three months ago, and yesterday. By husbanding his time, he would have made time work for him to produce business.

Your time must be organized to work *for* you and not *against* you!

Don't Be Like J.H.

J.H. kept a diary for his daily activities. It made him feel organized. However, J.H. made only what he felt were necessary calls—a few friends and acquaintances with whom he chatted away the day. They never took J.H. seriously because they felt that anyone who had time to chat with them all day couldn't be very busy or important. Since he was neither busy nor important, they did not give him business!

Community Work—Getting to Know the People Around You

Large cities are a collection of small communities. New York has the Murray Hill area, the Chelsea area, and many other sections. Other large cities have similar area breakdowns. The smaller cities and the suburban areas are, of course, small communities unto themselves. The registered representative who lives in a small town, as well as the one who lives in a large city, should indulge in community work. For the registered representative in the smaller town, participation in community work should be his main source of acquiring clients. He cannot make cold calls or mailings as readily as the representative in a large city, who has thousands or even millions of anonymous individuals to call upon. In joining organizations, do not blatantly announce that you are seeking business. Do the work of the group sincerely and effectively, and the members will come to you with no pressure on your part.

CHAPTER 2

TYPES OF INVESTORS

EACH INVESTOR IS AN INDIVIDUAL WITH SPECIFIC investment requirements. The least important factor in analyzing the investor's needs is the amount of money available for investment. The most important factor is his investment requirements. Chapter 9 discusses in detail the methods of analyzing investors in order to determine which securities are suitable for that individual. But, before becoming specific, let us take a look at investor types in general. We do not advise lumping individual investors together into one general category; rather, we are dealing in general types in much the same manner as the student of psychology, who will study the general before analyzing the individual. Likewise, the security analyst will divide stocks into broad categories, such as growth or income type, before making specific selections.

The investor types described are varied, and one individual may have some characteristics of each type. For example: a successful businessman may hold part of his portfolio in high grade securities, and thereby fall into the category of long-term investor. He may use another part of his portfolio for trading purposes, and thereby fall into the category of trader. Again we say, analyze the individual, but the beginnings of all specific analyses start with the general, and the registered representative must realize that he cannot be general, unless he continues on to the making of a specific individual analysis.

Prepare yourself to meet three basic types of investors: the trader, the semi-sophisticated investor, and the new investor. Learn their needs, wants, and requirements as well as their expectations of you. As is usual with all things in life, that which gives the greatest reward is the most difficult to obtain. The trader who can provide you with your largest source of income is the most difficult type of account to get.

The Trader Will Make Demands of You

The trader cannot afford to do business with anyone except a knowledgeable representative. You can't outsmart him, out-talk him, or make him in any way fail to see you for what you truly are. You will have to know your business thoroughly. You will have to be up-to-the-second in your awareness of the news. He wants facts quickly and accurately. As for opinions, he will listen but will not accept them unless they are sound and well-reasoned. When *he* has made an opinion, it has been based on facts which he has marshalled. You cannot change his opinion, unless you can provide and prove a different set of facts. When he asks you about a stock, chances are he has already done research in the situation and wants to know what you know about it. If you don't know much he won't hold it against you, and will probably be willing to give you a chance to get the facts together. He'll forgive you for not knowing, but he *won't* forgive you for not being able to gather information. He expects that you will know where and how to get the facts needed for forming an opinion.

Make sure anything you tell him is precise and up-to-the-minute. He doesn't want yesterday's news. He doesn't want vague conjecture about what may be, and any opinion must be based on specific correlated facts. He considers himself to be as knowledgeable or even more knowledgeable than you.

The Trader Is a Major Source of Potential Business

Chances are he is himself an astute, successful business or professional man. His keenness of mind is devoted to the analysis of business news. He is the complete realist. He sees things for what they are, and can evaluate all the possibilities in a situation. He will make tremendous demands of you. He is usually a man who is used to the best service in everything he does. You may carry out the first order he gives you while he sits in another board room to check your speed of execution. He undoubtedly has checked the quotation before he placed the order, and expects you to call him back immediately upon execution with a fresh quote.

The Trader Respects Your Opinions

I have not meant to imply that he will treat you as an inferior. To him you are an equal, and both of you are pooling your knowledge and abilities in order to make money for the client and commissions for yourself. If you don't come up to his standards, he won't give you business. If you meet his requirements you will get his business.

He will usually deal with a few brokers rather than with one. In this manner he can acquire information from various sources. The information he gets from one broker will be given to another broker for corroboration.

Because he mingles with other men like himself, he can refer excellent prospects to you, and if you service him well, you may quickly establish a substantial business for yourself, as did my friend D.E., who is now manager of a midtown branch. Six years ago, in the early part of his career, he called on a lead in an office building which was a distance away from his office. The man he met was a young, successful businessman. He liked D.E.'s aggressiveness and gave him a few trades, and then turned over his entire account. He subsequently referred substantial businessmen like himself to D.E., and provided him with an excellent account list.

The Trader Must Be Cultivated

The trader is very easy to meet, but hard to get. He is everywhere seeking information and ideas. You will meet him when you join a club, speak to a group, call on leads, or make cold calls. He will listen to what you have to say, and file it in his memory. Each time he talks to you he will mentally take down your opinions. After many such conversations, if your ideas have proven sound, he will start to do business with you.

He is shrewd enough to know that your selections cannot work out all the time. However, he expects that if a situation changes, you will be right on top of the change and act accordingly.

Do not look upon him as a hard task-master. He is only looking for those qualities in a broker which you yourself would seek if you were to need a broker.

He will buy any type security, from the blue chip to the low priced over-the-counter issue, as long as it has sound possibilities. He does not buy on whim or simply to take a chance. He is not a gambler hoping to beat the odds. He is a man who weighs the risks, and invests when the possibilities for gain outweigh the dangers. He will stay with the situation only as long as it has promise. When the promise has been fulfilled or has lost the possibility of being achieved, he will leave the situation. You will have to advise him of your opinion in either event.

The Long-Term Investor Represents Another Important Part of Your Business

In contrast with the speculator is the cautious long-term investor, who is seeking either growth over the years or a steady source of dividend income. He is usually semi-sophisticated about investing. A great many such accounts are women, but men will also fall into this category. Unlike the trader, these investors will rely chiefly on you as their source of information, and will abide by your selections. They will listen to your opinions, and are usually not equipped by knowledge or training to evaluate your opinions. They will accept your judgments at face value. Such confidence places a double burden on you. Your opinions must be well-founded and must be expressed in language understandable to the less sophisticated. Also, since your word is usually accepted without question, you have to live up to every high standard of ethical conduct demanded of the securities business.

Since you will for the most part be buying and selling high grade securities for the semi-sophisticated, some of the anxiety of making decisions about other people's money will be reduced. But demands will be made on you in other ways. You will have to answer many such questions as: "When was the dividend paid and how much was it?," "Should I sell my Jersey and buy Telephone?," or "I was talking to a friend who recommended XYZ—what do you think?" You will also be called innumerable times to discuss the market with someone who is living off her dividends and who has nothing better to do than call her broker each day.

Don't Lose Patience With the Semi-Sophisticated Investor

The servicing of the un-sophisticated account will make demands upon your patience. The many simple questions which you will have to answer will try your patience, as will the constant demands for information which lead only to a small order.

You will not be called at all by an investor whose

securities could use a re-evaluation. His stocks are in a vault where they cannot be touched or seen. When a long-term situation has worked out or has failed to work out, you will have difficulty in convincing this investor to change to a more promising situation. He tends to look upon his stocks as something to be put away and forgotten; he fails to realize the importance of investment supervision.

A Word of Caution About Conservative Investors

Beware of the long-term investor who suddenly decides to take up speculation. Many individuals start out conservatively, but, perhaps during a trip to a resort where they talk "stock market" with the other guests, they hear about someone who has made a fortune in Polaroid, Xerox, or Syntex. Upon their return, you are called upon to produce a similar miracle. Unlike our sophisticated trader, the conservative person who turns speculator is not a reasonable person. He is acting out of context to his true self, and although his new character role will mean considerable commissions, he is not to be encouraged in speculative undertakings. Sober him up by pointing out the wide fluctuations in these "high flyers," and how he may very well lose money as well as make it. The conservative person who turns speculator and loses money will never forgive you for the loss. He will say, "You should have stopped me." This remark may sound unreasonable. But it is not. As a person's broker, you are supposed to know that person not only financially, but also psychologically, in order to have good customer relations.

This Man Didn't Use Sound Judgment

G.L. is a registered representative in a walk-in office. He was approached by an elderly woman who invested her last $10,000 in speculative securities. Although she made profits in some of the choices, she lost money in others; on balance she was a little ahead, but the losses upset her. She went to see a partner about her account. He advised her to close out and remove the account from the firm, inasmuch as she should not engage in speculative transactions.

The long-term investor is a great responsibility, for he relies upon you to tell him what and when to buy. He seeks and needs your guidance. He can be an excellent source of radiation, because he mingles with others like himself. But should they refer accounts to you, you must be very careful about your recommendations. If you should recommend security "A" to one account and security "B" to another, you will have to answer to both, because they compare notes.

Since most retired people are long-term investors, and since they have plenty of time on their hands, they may very well call you for the most trivial information. You will have to exert diplomacy in order to keep the account and not appear rude as you strain to spend time with your more productive accounts. Although the account may be inactive, he will require periodic mailings of literature to keep him informed. He expects and even demands this attention.

Of the 1,000,000 New Investors Each Year, How Many Will Be Yours?

The new investor usually comes from the ranks of the younger groups. He may be a young investor just starting out on his career, or a promising young businessman seeking to augment his income by speculation. It may even be a middle-aged couple seeking to invest their savings for better income and growth possibilities, or a career woman who wishes to invest for her future security. Whoever the person or whatever the investment, it is *you* who are to inform and guide the account. They will look upon you as a knowledgeable and intelligent source of information. They may be relatively uninformed, but not stupid or gullible. They will be seeking information from various sources and will select that information which makes the most sense for them. They will not be speculators, but will probably want securities with growth as well as income possibilities.

The New Investor Takes Cultivation

The new investor, even from the young business and professional group, will take many call-backs before he becomes a customer. He will need to be educated in investments. Not knowing you, he will not quickly accept your recommendations but will want to learn for himself so that he may make a decision. You will have to provide that information which appears most suitable to his investment needs. Whenever possible, try to meet the new investor in person. He will have more confidence in a person he can see and hear than he will in a voice on the telephone. New investors are invariably small accounts at the start. Due to his caution, he will commit only a small part of the money he has available for investment.

You will need patience with the new investor—patience for him to open an account. You must not be disappointed when the amount invested is small. You will have to remember that each *new* account is the possible beginning of a *large* account. The new account can refer you to other accounts. The effort of opening a new account is worth the trouble, even if it is small.

The new investor is very much like a newly planted seed. Just as the seed develops underground out of sight, nurtured by the soil and water, and suddenly bursts out of the ground as a green plant, the new investor is absorbing the ideas you have given him and the literature you have sent him, and if you have provided the proper "investment nutrients," he too will flourish into a full-fledged account.

Don't Forget Dividends—the New Investor Likes Them

In the past 10 years, which have shown such great emphasis on growth of stocks, we have tended to forget the great hold which the concept of dividends exerts over the investing public. Even though your account is seeking profits, he invariably asks, "How much is the dividend?" No investor or trader is immune to this question. The speculator asks it as a guide to the profitability of the company. The investor asks it as a criterion of soundness of the company. Despite the tremendous amount of promotional material put out by the investment trade associations, explaining that a common stockholder is an owner of a company and that dividends are his participation in the company's profits, too many individuals still think of common stock ownership as a loan to the company for which they will receive a return. This false concept is prevalent among many new and unsophisticated investors, and the registered representative should make sure the proper concept is held by the investor. The power which dividends hold over the investor's imagination is not hard to comprehend when one thinks back to the earliest relationship one has with money. Most of us, early in our lives, had a bank account which our parents or grandparents started for us as a lesson in thrift. For the first time we received something called interest—money paid to us for the use of our money. Our next meeting with dividends may have come when we took out our first insurance policy; again, when we purchased Series E bonds, we received interest. Our idea of dividends had been established as something received for letting someone else use our money. We had not learned the difference between dividends and interest. The concept of growth was unknown, except that your money grew if you reinvested your dividends.

The new investor with this faulty understanding of dividends is hard-put to understand the concept of growth, and should be introduced to investing via the dividend-paying security. He will usually not understand the concept of corporate growth through reinvested earnings, and will only appreciate its potential upon becoming more sophisticated. You will find your job easier if you offer him a security with a dividend.

New Investors Like Mutual Funds and the M.I.P.

Many new investors enter the securities market through the purchase of mutual fund shares or the M.I.P. It is not the purpose of this book to discuss their relative merits, but the newly registered representative would do well to try to open accounts in either or both. The young executive who starts an M.I.P. plan today may become your trading account a few years hence when he becomes more affluent. The doctor who buys mutual fund shares today may be tomorrow's source of many new accounts. As the executive rises in business and the doctor's practice increases, your accounts will grow with them. Don't take the short-sighted outlook that an M.I.P. commission is too trivial to be concerned with, or that a mutual fund is a dormant account. Over the long term, and it is your intention to make this a lifetime career, the small investor can become the large investor, and be a source for innumerable accounts. Look at the new investor as your investment in your own future. He is not so much the source of today's business as he is the source of tomorrow's business.

He will take much of your time as he undergoes an educational process, and you will need to feed him educational material. Most of this can be in printed form, using the various pamphlets mentioned later in the book.

Basically, the newer account is won by proving that dividends and growth from common stocks, over the years, have proven more beneficial than dividends alone. Your rival for the new investor's money is the savings account at interest, or the savings and loan account. You might suggest shares in bank stocks or savings and loan stocks to such an investor! He can also be moved by being shown how inflation has eaten into his capital, and how savings at fixed income are not the entire answer to today's investment problems.

Many representatives have built their business by catering to new investors via mutual funds. H.M. started his career with a member firm through a mutual fund department. The people he met were mostly unsophisticated new investors. They liked the idea of diversification and investment management and so became investors. As they received the quarterly reports of the mutual funds and saw the reports of purchases and sales, they took a direct interest in the stock market and were soon placing orders for their own stock purchases with H.M., who now found himself dealing not only with mutual fund accounts, but also with active investors and even traders.

Of course, each investor should have a bank account and insurance before undertaking an investment program, and the registered representative must see to it that each account has these financial foundations before letting him invest in the securities market.

Don't Assume Knowledge of Investing on the Part of Your Customers

Strangely, experienced as well as neophyte investors have much misunderstanding and lack of knowledge as to how the securities market really works. A man who has been trading for 20 years may very well not have the knowledge you have, because he will lack the comprehensive training you have received. Do not be awed by the man who has been in the market since you were 10 years old. You may know more about how the securities market works than he does. Also, do not lose patience with the new investor for his lack of investment education. He will have some grave misconceptions, but it is your job to correct them.

Investors Need to Understand That Risk Is a Part of Investing

Whereas the experienced investor is prepared to accept reasonable risk, the new investor still needs to learn the place of risk in investing. His entire attitude can be formed by your representation of risk.

No one should invest unless he is willing to accept risk. There are different degrees of risk inherent in each type of security, but, whether large or small, it is always present. While it is your duty to point out the risks of investing, you may also point out that profits can only be made by taking some risk.

The person who is willing to accept the risks attendant upon seeking profits is your best customer. He is the person who instinctively knows that the greatness of this country came about through the doings of those who took risks. From those who founded the American Republic to those who established its industries—calculated risk has been in the best American tradition. The early fur trappers, the whaling ship crews, the farmers and ranchers, the gold prospectors, the oil field searchers, and the railroad men were in the forefront of those who made this country great. The purchase of common stocks is in that tradition. The early risk-takers gambled with their lives. Today's risk-takers are only obliged to risk money. It is also part of the American tradition that each man can become rich, and that tradition also includes the belief that he who is to grow rich must take chances and be resourceful.

Who are the risk-takers? They are, in the main, men who have established their own profitable businesses. In this group lie your best prospects for active accounts. The second-best group of risk-takers is the professional group. Many doctors and dentists find their jobs too routine. There is no challenge to them in their daily parade of patients, and they seek to match wits with the stock market. From the above-mentioned two groups may come your most important customers.

They will not be easy to solicit, and they will not be easy to keep, but where your *rewards* are potentially great, so are your *risks*.

Where the Greatest Rewards Are—The Institutional Account

Although we advocate that only the most knowledgeable and sophisticated registered representative seek out the institutional account (it is too unlikely a prospect for the new man), it is so large a business that it is worth going after. However, you should do so only after arduous preparation. Institutional business currently accounts for approximately 30 per cent of N.Y.S.E. volume annually, and has every expectation of growing.

Don't waste your time going to the institutions for business directly, unless you are prepared to go back again and again, and even then with no assurance of success. One method of getting institutional business is by seeking it among the individuals you contact. (You will be calling literally hundreds of people through the years.)

As you seek out individuals for business, ascertain whether they have connections with institutional accounts which you can utilize. It is useless to go to the institutional investor unless your material has been the result of exhaustive research and is being offered to them uniquely. Don't make a few random phone calls in the hopes of striking an order. The institutions maintain their own order rooms and their personnel have strict instructions about the placement of orders. They do not give out orders at random, but usually to a prepared list of brokerage firms. You will need to get on the list in order to be eligible for business.

The way to get on the list is to prove to the institutional customers that you can provide them with a sound and thoroughly researched situation which they can use. If you have the capabilities for independent research, and can marshal your material into an effective presentation, then, by all means, call on the institutional manager. Although being a registered representative is a difficult job, servicing the institutions is more difficult. You will be dealing with men whose knowledge of securities is among the best in the country. You cannot just whip together some ideas and offer them as research. You will need to do intensive analysis. It would be prudent to prepare yourself for institutional sales by taking courses in Security Analysis.

As you can see, working on institutional accounts takes away time from working on smaller, individual investors. If you decide to work on institutions, you are banking on making big sales only. There will not be time for smaller accounts. If you have the capabilities, your firm will cooperate with you by allowing you to work closely with the research department. But don't expect to close those large sales immediately. The experience of S.S. is typical of the patience needed to solicit institutional business.

S.S., who had a B.S. degree in Economics, decided to go after institutional business. He pointed out to his firm the possibilities of getting labor union accounts. His firm agreed to assist him in a campaign to get that business. S.S. did research work and wrote to, called on, and canvassed the various labor unions. After many months, business started to trickle in. After two years it was a substantial amount, and now, after three years, S.S. receives a sizable volume of business. Of course, he maintains constant service to the accounts.

Institutional accounts include banks, insurance companies, mutual funds, unions, and universities.

The mutual funds are of many varieties and if your research turns up an interesting situation, you may find a mutual fund to which your selection is suitable. Try to see the portfolio manager in person to present your story. Don't mail out the information in hopes of a reply. Like every one else, he is quite busy and may not get to the report for a while. Like every hard-to-see person, however, if he is approached cordially and professionally, he will probably find time to see you. Make a trip out of town to see a fund manager in another city. Anyone who is willing to come several hundred miles to see him will be greeted cordially! But call first to arrange an appointment.

The same holds true for the banks. The man to see is the investment manager. After many courteous calls, he will talk to you. You may have to make many calls and stand for many delays, but sooner or later he will see you. He may not buy at first, but establish your relationship and you may add a substantial account to your books.

Don't Be Overanxious for Business

One more type merits our attention—the troublesome customer. This business is a difficult one. Don't make your life more difficult by dealing with individuals who are potential troublemakers. Trouble is bound to come from any customer to whom rash promises have been made as to a stock's potential. Trouble will come from the customer who was pressured into buying by constant calls and strong statements.

Many individuals are congenital troublemakers. Even though they are aware of the risks in investing, they will, if a stock declines, seek to blame the broker and thereby recoup the loss. It is difficult to ascertain which person will react in this fashion. Watch out in your soliciting for those who are argumentative or overly critical, and for those who buy too easily. (One can buy easily if one intends to pay only if the stock goes up!)

Look out for the new account who gives you a large order. The new registered representative is fair game for the swindler, and there are individuals who lie awake nights scheming how to swindle brokerage firms. Their easiest entree is through the new man who, anxious to do business, will eagerly accept the large order designed as a trap for the neophyte. If the stock goes up, the customer will pay—if not, you pay. Or the large order may be a means to "paint the tape."

Rule 405, the "Know Your Customer" Rule of the New York Stock Exchange, and the Rules of Fair Practice of the N.A.S.D. are broad in their implications. The responsibility for each account rests with you and your firm. But since you make the initial contact with the account, it is incumbent upon you to weed out the "trouble account." The Rules go beyond learning the essential facts about each customer. They include finding out the investment needs of each customer and selecting those securities suitable for his needs.

No Matter the Size of the Account, Analyze His Needs

These, then, are the people you will meet: people with varying investment requirements. Find out their needs, analyze their financial abilities, and select those securities suitable for their individual needs. Customers know the difference between the man who sells for the sake of selling and the man who makes a selection in line with their needs. Sincerity of purpose is the best way to establish and hold accounts. We will further discuss analyzing the customer's needs later, for therein lies the key to your success.

CHAPTER 3

BUILDING YOUR GENERATOR

SUCCESS COMES FROM AN INNER DESIRE TO WORK and to succeed. The successful do not need someone to prod them, push them, or cajole them into action. Paul Getty could have retired when he was 24 years old, with considerable wealth; but the desire to achieve greater heights was within him. The folklore of our business world is full of stories of men who drove themselves to success. But before you set out on the road to high earnings, you must map out your trip.

The trip is not non-stop; sometimes you will move rapidly, sometimes slowly. What is important is that you know where you are going. Where do you want to be six months from now? Do you want 50 accounts at the end of six months? Do you want 100 accounts at the end of a year? Then you can plan as L.F. did.

[32]

L.F. set a goal of 100 accounts by the end of his first year in business. This meant two accounts a week. He planned his daily work to meet this objective. At the end of the first year he had 120 accounts. At one point, for a full month, he opened an account a day!

Try to Build a Surplus of Goals

Goals must be realistic and yet should somewhat exceed your abilities. If you set too easy a goal for yourself, you will be cheating yourself.

Realistically, first year goals should range from 50 to 100 accounts, and first year goals' net commissions should range from $4000 to $8000. The range of difference is due to the fact that one man may be slow to get started; by the third year, if they work diligently, they should pull about even.

For the first two months, try to reach a minimum goal of six new accounts a month; eight accounts a month in the following two months; then ten a month for the next four months; and twelve a month for the last four months. Keep a memo of this goal on your desk in front of you.

Make Stamina One of Your Fixed Assets

These goals, although realistic, will not be easy; but by reaching out beyond yourself, you will achieve more. No one knows his true potential, and you will amaze yourself with how much you accomplish if you are really determined.

Those of you who have served in the Army or Navy know that each of us is capable of more than he thinks he can do. In the Army, no sooner did you collapse from exhaustion, than the order came to march, and you found yourself covering another mile.

In a sense, building your business is like being in a war. You cannot indulge yourself or try to do it the easy way. There is no easy way. The rewards are only there for those who exert themselves beyond normal limits.

By giving yourself a difficult goal to reach each month, you will drive yourself to attain it. Watch out for sideroads and detours which keep you off the main route. Do only those things which are needed to attain your objective.

The older men entering the business usually will use time to their best advantage, like R.J. who is today a partner in a medium-sized member firm. When he entered the securities business 12 years ago, he brought with him a determination to succeed, because he was at that time 45 years old and felt his energies would decline as he grew older. He had to do it now or never. Whether or not his belief was true is not the point. His belief gave him a reason to set goals for himself. He wished to see an accomplishment each month. He wanted to make sure that his energies were being used wisely. As he progressed, he set higher goals. Today, he is looking forward to further expansion of the firm.

Keep Your Stated Value in Front of You

The younger man also needs to know the value of time. Keep a memo of the goal in front of you, on your desk pad. Each day, check your results against your goal. If you're behind, step up your pace. If you're ahead, keep up the good work.

Remember, make your goal higher than you actually believe you can attain. Setting high standards will cause you to work harder in order to achieve those standards.

It is not easy to be one's own master. We like to go easy on ourselves and to take the path of least resistance. Each of us has a tendency to do things which look like work but which are not really work. We are too prone to delude ourselves into believing we are working, when in reality we are not. It is so easy and pleasant to get into the office at 9:55, take a good hour for lunch and leave at 3:40 and then go home and tell the wife about your hard day at the office. But unless you are blessed with rich relatives, don't try to make a living this way, because even they will begin to feel that someone more conscientious should be watching their investments.

Capitalize on Your Efforts

We need to know that which is productive effort from that which is non-productive. We also need to know the grades of importance of the kinds of productive effort. As a guide, here is a list of productive efforts in their *descending* order of importance:

1. Making sales
2. Talking to customers
3. Research work
4. Talking to prospects
5. Prospecting by phone or mail
6. Self-evaluation
7. Watching the tape

Non-productive and unnecessary efforts include:

1. Watching the tape if one has no customers
2. Idle talk with other registered representatives
3. Long lunches and coffee breaks

Ask yourself during the day: "Is what I am doing now really productive?" In this way you will spot check on yourself in much the same way that a foreman checks on a worker. Again remember, you must be both foreman and worker.

The Three Worst Liabilities You May Incur

LIABILITY #1: *Ticker Hypnotism*

The person so afflicted gets so engrossed in the tape that he neglects to make calls. Actually, he uses the excuse of watching the ticker as a reason for not working. Those hypnotized by the ticker are willingly so. It is a good way to make believe one is working. This person will, from time to time, give evidence of consciousness by shouting out "Look at that stock go up!" or "down" as the case may be, but these blurtings are his only communications with the outside world while seemingly entranced by the tape. Another representative, similarly smitten, will keep a chart of each tick of certain issues, and will be virtually incommunicado, while making constant notes on his pad. Watching the ticker is not really working. One should look at the ticker in the same way that one can listen to a radio while working in a shop. The ticker is not for one's exclusive attention. It is the background music, so to speak, for your work, but it is not your work itself. The representative who is engrossed in the ticker is shirking the real hard work necessary to get accounts, and will not survive in the securities business. It is all well and good to say, "I have to see what is going on in the market so that I can tell my customers." But first things come first, and customers are always first.

"Ticker hypnotism" has been the downfall of many would-be representatives. An extreme case of this is illustrated by V.B., who had an interest in statistics. He found them more interesting than people. His college grades were excellent, and he passed the Registered Representative examination with an "A." V.B. spent most of his time watching and recording trends off the tape. He became very good at interpreting the tape but was unable to develop customers because his analytical studies took all his time. His father-in-law offered to buy him a seat. He accepted, expecting to employ his analytical studies to assist him in trading for his own account. However, he found that keeping active on the floor was not to his liking. He preferred to devote his time to charting. He subsequently sold the seat, and now trades for his own account as a customer. V.B. needed to learn how to communicate with people, which is equally as important for the registered representative as interpreting the tape.

LIABILITY #2: *Spending Time in Conversation with Other Representatives in the Board Room*

Because the board room atmosphere is very informal, and because you are in close proximity with other registered representatives, it is easy to fall into the pattern of carrying on conversations with those around you. Inasmuch as the other men in the office will never open an account with you, it hardly seems profitable to talk to them. You may condone such conversations by calling them an "exchange of ideas," but what may start out as a casual talk easily becomes a daily pattern of behavior, simply because it is easier to do than work. Of course, an exchange of ideas is part of your job, but not to the exclusion of seeking and servicing accounts.

Board room conversations, if taped and played back to the representative, would end all further conversations because they all sound like this:

> I told my customer to buy it at 29. (It is now 34.)
> That stock looked like a short sale last week. I knew it.
> Do you think they'll raise (or lower) the discount rate?
> The market looks (choose one) high, strong, low, weak, ready to fall, ready to rise, uncertain.
> How can you (choose one) buy, sell, trade, in this market?
> It's a (choose one) Buy, Sale Short.
> These (choose one) leads, accounts, reports are no good.
> I made three calls today and everyone is on vacation.

If you find yourself seeking out other representatives to talk with, the reason usually is that you are either not sure of yourself or are reluctant to work. If you are not too sure of yourself, go to your manager for guidance. If you are reluctant to work, do not stay in the business. If other men seek you out for conversation and thereby deprive you of your time, tell them they are wasting both your time and their own. It is better to have a great many accounts than to be popular with other men in the office.

LIABILITY #3: *Is the Illusion of Work Attained by Reading Research Reports in the Office?*

You are not working if you read reports or the Wall Street Journal in the office after the opening. The time can better be spent in the soliciting of accounts through phone calls or in seeking out prospects. You read only when you cannot reach or do not *try* to reach people.

There is nothing more wasteful than the reading of newspapers and reports during those hours when customers and prospects can be reached. Research, of course, is part of your job; allot the evening hours to research. If you read reports at 10 A.M., you will antagonize clients by calling them at 10 P.M. Again, this is the illusion of work and not work itself.

Here Are Some Less Important Liabilities

There are other time-wasters which exist outside your office. In your social life—which must now be an extension of your business life—make sure to mingle with those people who can become accounts. You are not spending your social life productively if you are not meeting and mingling with potential customers.

Time Is Your Most Important Asset

Together with setting goals, the representative must have a built-in sense of the value of time. Each moment of the day must be spent in a productive effort. Think of yourself as a machine in a manufacturing plant. If you stand idle, you make nothing. If you run properly for 10 hours a day, you turn out sizeable commissions; so it is important to keep yourself running efficiently for as many hours as possible. You can train yourself to be an efficient working machine. Give yourself a daily reminder. Here's how one man paced himself:

H.N. worked in spurts. He could not maintain a sustained effort. One day, as his wife prepared his eggs using a timer shaped as an hour-glass, he got an idea. He bought an hour-glass at a gift shop and placed it on his desk. He worked to meet the demands of the running sands of time. The sight of the sand constantly running through the glass gave him a sense of time. H.N. had taken an abstract idea like time and had made it work for him.

Your Current Assets Are: Time, Work, and Knowledge

You, too, must think of time as one of your most important tools. Along with your knowledge and energy, it is one of the three cornerstones for building your business. Whether we come from rich, poor, or average backgrounds, we are all born with certain abilities and we are all given the gift of time. In time, the rich man can dissipate his wealth, and the poor man can attain riches. It is what each of us *does* with his energy, ability, and time that is important. Since childhood, we have heard the axiom, "time is money." Like most of our proverbial sayings, we disregard this as an old cliché. And yet, if you think of it as a new saying, it rings true. How you spend your time will determine whether you'll have money to spend.

What Is Your "Net Worth"?

Stop right now and think! How much is your time worth? How much do you believe you should earn in a year? If you answer $10,000 then your time is worth $5 an hour, based on a forty-hour week. If your answer is $15,000 then your time is worth $7.50 an hour. But saying that your time is worth $7.50 an hour is one thing, and doing those things which will earn that money for you is another. Your time will only turn to money if you do those things which will make money.

How to Raise Your Personal "Margin of Profit"

You need to develop within you a *time-value sense.* This means thinking of time as being so valuable that you cannot afford to lose any of it. If you dropped a half-dollar down a grating, you would resent your own carelessness. You should have the same feeling about lost or wasted time. If you do not have this time-value sense you will need to develop it, because, unfortunately, no one will sit beside you and tell you what to do or tell you if what you are doing is productive. This you must do yourself, and your success or failure hinges on your ability to determine what is and what is not productive. Can you conceive of anyone paying you $5 an hour to talk to the man at the desk next to you? Can you see anyone paying you $10 an hour just to sit in an office and look at the ticker tape? Will anyone pay you $7.50 an hour to sit around and read newspapers? Of course not! So why do any of these unproductive activities?

Time is your most precious commodity. Don't defraud yourself into losing time in unprofitable pursuits. Don't let others steal time from you.

As you progress in the securities business, your time will become more and more valuable. Just like the doctor who starts his practice by charging $5 a call and then progresses to $15 and $20, you too will expect more of a return on your time. As your abilities sharpen and your knowledge increases, you *will* get higher "fees" for your services in the form of increased commission.

You will not be alone if your first year's earnings are low, so do not be disappointed. Look at W.E., who entered the securities business with high ambitions but earned only $6,000 his first year. He told a partner of his disappointment. The partner told him he'd earned only $4,000, and that it wasn't the first year's earnings which are important. What *is* important is establishing a pattern for working, which W.E. had done. In his next year W.E. earned $10,000 and is currently averaging $20,000.

Plan to Increase Your Operating Ratio

Planning your day will help you use your time productively. A planned day will impose a discipline upon you. If you are unable to discipline yourself from within, the planned day will be a form to guide you. Know in advance what you will be doing each hour of the day. Appoint a set time each day or week to put your plan into writing. At the end of each day's plan, indicate your goal for that day, so that you have before you both your plan and your goal.

At the end of each day, review your accomplishments. This doesn't have to be done in writing. Simply take a few minutes in quiet to think to yourself, "What did I accomplish today which gets me nearer to my goal?" "Am I satisfied with the amount of work I accomplished, or can I do better?" Then ask yourself, "If I were my boss, what would I pay myself for today's work?"

Can You Pass the "Acid Test"?

Here is the "acid test" of your work habits. Be objective. Would you really pay yourself for the day's work just done? You will need to be capable of self-evaluation. Don't waste your time in self-criticism or in self-deprecation. Only a positive attitude will help you. What are your true capabilities? Are you ready, willing, and able to work twelve hours a day? Can you make calls without being thrown back by rebuffs and disappointment? Can you absorb the tremendous amount of research material needed to do your job properly? Can you define the investment objectives of the various types of clients? Can you take the frustrations of dull markets? Can you handle the job with calm and dispatch and meet the demands made by very active markets? Are you sure your client's interest will always be foremost in your mind? What if the stocks you have recommended do not do as anticipated? Will you fold up and quit, or will you analyze the reason why and make whatever changes are necessary? Will you know how to pace yourself so that you don't overdo your job and become too tired to work properly? If you get a few very active accounts, will you then stop looking for new business? If you acquire only small accounts and don't seem to be able to land the big ones, will you give up in disgust? Self-evaluation is a never-ending business. As you reach each new plateau in the progress of your career, stop and question how you may best use your abilities to continue onward and upward.

Check Your "Ratios"

Self-evaluation means judging not only your abilities, but also your worth in earning power. Realistically ask yourself "What should I be earning?" (Not, "What would I like to earn," but "What should I earn based upon my efforts and abilities?")

If you are working as hard as the man next to you and he is earning twice as much as you, what are you doing wrong? Why is each order that he places worth $30 while yours are worth only $15?

In a manufacturing plant, a time-study engineer is called in to keep the work pace going properly. You will need to be your own time-study engineer.

Check over these "performance ratios." Are they in line with your own?

Do you call at least 10 suspects a day?

Do you send out at least 25 mailing pieces a day?

Do you waste time talking at length to unpromising prospects?

Do you give an account more attention than he requires?

Do you give an account less attention than he requires?

Do you spend at least three hours a week in planning and organizing your work?

Do you spend at least two hours a week in making cold calls?

Do you add at least 10 new suspects to your list each day?

Do you ask each prospect and account for referrals?

Do you read research reports critically, with an eye to making selections for the needs of specific prospects and customers?

Do you review each account at least once a month?

Do you call dormant accounts once a month to find out about any change in their circumstances?

Do you engage in community work at least twice a month?

Do you cultivate the friendship of those capable of doing business with you?

Do you make sure to offer M.I.P., Mutual Funds, Options, and Bonds as well as Stocks?

Are you satisfied with your progress?

The self-evaluation phase of your work is most important. Place it on your list as something *you must do* to become successful. Self-evaluation will tell you how powerfully or weakly your "generator" is operating.

CHAPTER 4

RECORD-KEEPING

RECORD-KEEPING MAY SEEM LIKE A TEDIOUS bore to a dynamic individual, but it is essential to the proper servicing of accounts, and it is a main source of business. Exact and complete records impose the necessary framework within which you can work effectively. When a stock shows unusual market activity, you will already have a record of each customer who owns that stock. You will be able to call each one quickly with your recommendation. Upon reading a news item which may influence the movement of a stock, you will know at once which prospects and customers to notify.

You will not be at a loss as to what to do in each situation. Record-keeping will pre-arrange each move for you, and each move will be correct and accurate.

[46]

Here is a list of records you must keep:

1. Blotter of Buy and Sell orders entered for the day.
2. Account's record of trades.
3. Stock record with holdings for each account.
4. Card file containing all pertinent data about the account.
5. Daily diary.
6. Prospect cards.
7. "Suspect" list.

Buy and Sell Blotter

The *blotter of buy and sell orders* keeps track of your daily business. Should an order not be executed, you will have a record of the order being entered and can tell the account that the order was not executed and ask for a new order. Where the order was executed you will, of course, call and advise the customer of the execution. You should, at this time, also ask the customer to send his check as promptly as possible.

By watching the blotter and the tape you can suggest to your customers that they change the prices of their orders, if necessary. Enter each order on the blotter immediately after writing the order ticket. The blotter can be a sheet of paper specially prepared for the purpose, or just a legal yellow pad. In your early months, with few orders coming in, the buy and sell blotter may seem superfluous, but the acquiring of good work habits must start early. As you get busier and busier, the blotter will act as a control over your daily business. It will keep you from making errors, and will assist you in making sales.

Account Record

The *account's record of trades* will give you the current position of the account as well as the past record of "buys" and "sells," with the profits and/or losses made in each transaction. This record will enable you to establish the profit and loss position of the account, the current position of the account, and the buying power in the account.

You will need to refer to record of trades constantly in order to evaluate the account's position and to recommend changes—but only where desirable. You will also need it to answer many of the questions your customer will ask about his account. Most important will be questions about dividends, and whether a trade was long-term or short-term, gain or loss.

It will also back you up when a customer calls who is dissatisfied with your handling of his account; you can point to the high spots—those investments which worked out favorably as contrasted with those which did not.

Stock Record Form

The *stock record form* will be a list of all your customers with holdings in the same stock, and the number of shares owned. For example, there will be one sheet for Bethlehem Steel—each account listed with the number of shares owned. Should any news appear about Bethlehem, you will call the list of customers immediately to inform them of the new developments and of your recommendation as to whether they should buy, hold, or sell.

If Bethlehem shows unusual activity, call the accounts

to inform them of the news. Your calls, which show you are watching the accounts, will be appreciated.

Account File by Alphabet

Maintain a card file by alphabet for each account, giving all pertinent data as to position, earnings, holdings, marital status, etc. The following is a sample card. The purpose of the *account file* card is to keep up-to-date on his financial position and on his financial requirements so that you may service the account properly.

ACCOUNT CARD

Name _____ Home _____ Phone _____
Business _____ Job _____ Phone _____
Income _____ No. of children _____ Ages _____
Investment objectives: _____
Personal interests: _____

The Daily Diary

The *daily diary* can be either your desk calendar or a special book in which you will record your required calls and appointments for the day. The daily diary is the focal point for your prospecting activities and for servicing of accounts. You will need to keep it neat and up-to-the minute. Without a daily diary you will be hopelessly disorganized. (It is also an excellent record for proving sales expenses deductions for income tax purposes.)

The daily diary is the key to your workday. It tells you whom to call and when. In it you will place notes of each call. These notes will then be transferred to the record kept for each account and prospect. A daily diary page will look like this:

Time	Name	No.	Reason For Call	Comments
9:15	Dr. Ben Seward	TI5-6217	Portfolio Analysis	Send analysis form and call back.
9:30	Philip Bender	GU9-4316	Mutual Fund	College Plans —Send growth fund.
9:45	Mrs. Carew	BU7-4219	Dividend Payers	Send list of Div. Paying stocks.
10:30	Jack Crown	FE3-2212	Market Opening	Call if C hits 62. Will place order.
11:00	R. Black	MO2-9279	Lead	No real interest.
11:15	G. Varet	NE9-3619	Referred by Simpson	Call in 6 mos.
11:30	Kay Greene	LO5-9919	Interest in XRX	Call if XRX drops to 200.
11:45	Dr. Fred Turner	ES4-2929	Keogh, bill	Send Keogh lit. Call back.
12:00	L. Maxson	UL3-7369	MIP Plan	See Tues. night for plan.
2:15	V. Graymar	TE6-7432	Second call back	Says ins. stocks overpriced.

2:30	Z. Agrippa	VU1-0420	Friend of Lou Varet	Send sample portfolio $5,000.
2:45	J. Burns	RE4-6174	Tax exempts	Not in high enough tax bracket.
3:00	R. Wertz	BE3-4377	Friend of Lou Varet	See Wed. night at his home.
4:00	Dr. S. Gary	TU2-9497	Coppers	Has several brokers— place on mailing list.

The minimum number of calls listed on the diary page should be 10, and ideally should be 20.

The Prospect Card

The notes and comments which appear in the diary will be transferred to the *prospect card.* The prospect card is the embryo from which the account card will evolve. Initially it will be a name and address. As you make calls upon your prospect, it will be a record of those calls and the points discussed. You will also record whatever information you gather about the prospect himself.

The prospect card will contain all the information required of the Account Card, but will have on its back spaces on which to keep a record of calls made to the prospect. Those spaces may look like the following:

Date of Call	Comments
2/6/65	Owns X, M, International Wire, Lear. Has loss in Int. Wire & Lear. Recommend sale of both. Call back 2/13.
2/13/65	Doesn't want to take loss. Wait and see. Recommended switch to SRY. Call 2/20.
2/20/65	SRY up 1/2. Lear down 1/2. Advised switch. Call back 2/23.
2/23/65	Pointed out tax loss benefits. Place limit order to buy SRY. Sell Lear. Credit ref. 2nd Nat. Bank.

The "Suspect" List

The *"suspect" list* is a running list of names you have gathered as possible investors. You will be gathering names from many sources, and it is best to keep a small notebook on your person at all times in which to write names which come to your attention.

The suspect list is the one great source from which the new representative's future business will come. Its function is roughly analogous to that of a minor league baseball team, for it is from this group of prospects that you must determine which are going to develop into "winners." You will find that most of these eligibles will ultimately not be suitable, so in order to make your effort pay off, you must be sure to have a long list of "suspects."

The suspect list can be maintained on a legal yellow pad. The suspects should be broken down into categories based on the best means to approach them; by mail, by telephone, or a combination of both.

Prove Your Tax Deductions

Another important record, not directly needed for doing business but which has a money value, is a record of your daily expenses, for income tax purposes. Any legitimate expense incurred for the production of business is tax deductible; however, the burden of proof is upon you. Keep a daily expense record, preferably in a small diary specifically for that purpose. Expenses will include carfare, taxis, lunches and other entertainment, phone calls, financial publications, and other miscellaneous items. Armed with this list of expenses, if and when you are called by the Internal Revenue, you will be able to prove your case. Otherwise, your tax bill will be that much higher.

Keeping all of the preceding records may appear to be a tedious job. It *is*. But it is also a necessary job. At first it will help you to make customers; later, it will help you to keep customers. But above all, it will provide the guideposts to help you attain your goals.

EXHIBIT II.

Well Built Automobile Co.

Name	Number of Shares
E. Jones	10 Shares
J. Smith	100 "
M. Brown	50 "
G. Georges	75 "

EXHIBIT I.

Client Joseph N. Jones   Home Phone IE 6-4156

Home Address 231 Elm St., New City, N.Y.

Bus. Address 350 Main St., New City, N.Y.   Bus. Phone IE 7-1000

Name of Power of Attorney (if any)

Investment Objective Long Term Growth

Special Instructions Tfr. Stock—Send proceeds of sales

Description	Bought			Sold			Approximate		
	Date	No. of Shares	Price	Date	No. of Shares	Price	Profit	Loss	
XYZ	1/9/59	10	42½	1/7/62	10	52½	100		
ABD	7/9/59	20	32						D
FGH	2/4/62	30	48						D
DEF	9/8/62	50	35						D

SAMPLE RECORD FORMS

CHAPTER 5

THE SALE'S PROCESS

ACQUIRING ACCOUNTS IS A SIX STEP PROCESS, AND you, the representative, must master every one of the steps. They are:

The Pre-Approach . . . . . . (Suspect)
The Approach
The Interview . . . . (Prospect)
The Analysis
The Presentation
The Order . . . . (Customer)

Practice Due Diligence

The *pre-approach* is the accumulation of the names of potential investors and all the available information you can gather about the names. The job is similar to that of an intelligence agent. It requires diligence and a constant awareness that this is a total business

[55]

—which means that it is a business where you are always working, even when not behind your desk. Where a man lives provides information about him; his clubs, his hobbies, and his profession all lend to our knowledge of the potential investor. We must also ascertain the best way to contact our suspect. The pre-approach is in the nature of a scouting expedition which tells us whom we are to contact and how we are to contact him. Examples of pre-approach methods appear in later chapters.

Converting the Suspect to a Prospect

The *approach* is selecting and using the best method to reach the suspect. The varieties of approaches are numerous, and each approach should be suitable for the particular suspect. Mail, phone calls, cold calls, lectures, and advertisements are the main, broad methods of approach, but these methods must be specifically tailored to suit each suspect.

A Sample Approach

Let us presume a list of "suspects" who are all similar in some respect, let us say by profession. Let us go on to presume that we have a list of accountants. Our approach should thus have an appeal to accountants. Reflecting for a moment, taxes seem a likely approach; so we provide ourselves with information about securities with an interesting tax-saving feature. There are many such securities, but it is not our purpose to go into them here. Suffice it to say that we now have material with which to approach these suspects. Our next step is to decide whether we should mail the information with a reply card, call on the phone, or make cold calls. We must analyze the work habits of accountants. They spend a great deal of time out of their offices, but always leave a number at which they can be reached. A cold call may not find them in, and mail may be neglected. The best approach appears to be a phone call offering information for their study.

The same method of analysis must be used for each suspect list, and you must be aware of all the various materials which your firm, the Stock Exchange, the Mutual Funds, and other sources provide.

Some suspects may require a combination of approaches, and even a sequence of several methods. For example, members of a group to whom you have given a lecture should be followed up individually by mail.

The approach also includes maintaining contact with someone who has shown an interest, but who has not given you an interview. We must interpose here our definition of "interview," which is verbal contact with a suspect either in person or by phone, during which you are provided with the information necessary to analyze the person's investment requirements.

Anyone who has shown some interest, but who has not as yet become a prospect, can be approached, in the main, through mailings. You have noticed how certain magazines will send you mailing after mailing, even though you never reply. They know from experience that it may take as many as seven mailings to get a response. Your name is on their list because it was selected as a good possibility as a subscriber. You have to adopt the same attitude with your list of suspects who have shown a modicum of interest but whom you have been unable to convert to accounts. Keep approaching them with mailing pieces on a regularly-scheduled basis—twice a month is sufficient— and make periodic phone calls as a follow-up. Never throw away a name which has had the slightest interest. Should a name get one piece of mail in six months, do even that much. The circumstances of people are always changing, and many are curious about investing but do not then have the means. Others have the means and are afraid. Over a period of time, the man without money may get some, and the man with fear may lose his fright. You may be pleasantly surprised to acquire an account from what had seemed a dead source, old lists of names.

Qualifying the Prospect

The *interview* can be a meeting between you and prospect in your office, in his home, or in his office. It can also be one or more telephone conversations. The purpose of the interview is to gather all the information needed to service the account properly. It is also a time to establish a rapport with the customer-to-be, and to establish an understanding of his emotional make-up. Many people, although they both can afford to and would like to speculate, are not emotionally stable enough to take the hazards of speculation. A falling stock can cause them to go into a dither, and the problem of maintaining their equilibrium will fall upon you, their representative. Unless you are prepared to act as a wet nurse during such trying periods, suggest to the emotional types that they stay with the blue chips. We cannot define the characteristics which make an agreeable or disagreeable customer; but as you proceed in the business you will learn about the emotional make-up of people and also learn how to work with them. We will provide some broad guides to this problem later, but your best guides will come through experience.

Make Mistakes—They Help Too

The *interview* is not a one-sided affair. You are going to be judged by the prospect even more critically than he will be judged by you. Your first interviews will be most difficult, and in them you will make mistakes. After each interview, make a brief memo of what transpired so that you can review for any possible errors on your part, or for something you did which proved effective. In subsequent interviews, do not repeat the same mistakes. If you continue to make the same mistakes over and over, you don't belong in the business. Since you are also being judged, do not: (a) offer snap opinions, (b) have ready answers, (c) act overbearingly, or (d) appear professional to the point of having a cold, clinical attitude. Where you do not know an answer, say so, but also say that you will get the answer through research.

Take notes during the interview. They help you with your customer analysis, and the act of writing keeps the attention of the other person focused upon you. It also shows you are interested enough in the person to keep a record of his conversation.

Do not try to make a sale at any time during the interview. This would be like a doctor prescribing medicine before he has finished examining the patient. The prospect will suspect your motives, and rightly so, and you will lose his interest. It is only after the interview that you have a true prospect or potential customer.

Pin-Pointing Objectives

The *analysis* takes place in the privacy of your home or office. You will collect all the information about the account, preferably on the *account analysis card,* a sample of which is on page 69. Every bit of pertinent information about the account is to be found on that card. You will now be able to give the prospect the best information, suitable to his personal needs and those of his family and his business. You will be able to ask for assistance from your superiors in the firm and your research department. They are sure to have suggestions which you can incorporate into the proposal you will set before the prospect. A sample analysis is given in a later chapter.

You Almost Have a Customer

The *presentation* can, like the interview, take place face-to-face or can be done by phone. The presentation should only be made after careful preparation. However, at least one of the two, the interview or the presentation, should take place on a personal basis. At least one face-to-face meeting with your prospect is important, mainly because it helps him to have confidence in you. It makes you tangible to the prospect—you are not just a disembodied voice. Simply stated, he'd rather invest with someone he can see than with someone he cannot see. The presentation can be in a written form prepared and approved by your research department, or a series of notes gathered by yourself and approved by your reseach department which you will present orally. In any event, be sure to check out your presentation with the research department, and in making your presentation orally, be sure to conform to all the standards for written and oral material required by the ethics of the business.

The purpose of the presentation is: (a) to show to the prospect your analysis of his financial situation, (b) to get his approval of your analysis, (c) to present your studied opinions for meeting his needs, and (d) to get his approval for your suggestions to open his account with you, based upon your analysis of and solution to his investment needs.

The Final Step: Getting the Account

The *order* is the opening of an account with you. One would logically conclude that proper analysis and presentation would lead to an order; it does not necessarily do so. We have been writing of a logical sequence of events which any rational being would accept as leading to one conclusion—a satisfied account. But we are dealing with people. You can make out the most precisely correct portfolio for an individual, and yet he won't buy—we have yet to deal with his emotions. If he is afraid to invest, no amount of logic will sway him. You can accomplish nothing unless the prospect has a feeling of confidence in you. Unfortunately, cold logic does not create confidence. What creates confidence is the feeling of rapport you create with the prospect. The sales process is like an egg—it can only be hatched by the warmth of your personal qualities.

The Spanish word *simpatico* best describes the feeling you should achieve. It means that you extend to this person a complete understanding of himself, not just as a customer, but as a fellow human being; that you are not seeking him out as someone to earn money on, but as someone whom you wish to help. He resents, just as you would, someone using his money just to earn commissions. He appreciates, just as you would, someone helping him with a serious problem. No one resents paying for proper assistance. Always look for and speak from the prospect's best interests—they are also your own. The individual with whom you establish this rapport will always be your customer, through good and bad markets.

Therefore, it will also behoove you to take an interest in your prospects' and accounts' personal affairs. What are their hopes for their children? What are their dreams for retirement? Where do they prefer to vacation? Why not send each account a birthday card? What problems do they have in their business? Speak of your personal wishes too. They are sure to be similar to theirs. You will then have a mutual understanding with each of them—you will be *simpatico*.

Only within this framework of personal warmth can you get and hold the account. This is the ingredient which binds the six steps of the sales process and establishes for you both the order and the account.

CHAPTER 6

PROSPECTING

IT IS NOT BY ACCIDENT THAT THE TERM USED BY salesmen for seeking out customers is "prospecting." The prospector is ordinarily thought of as one seeking riches through the discovery of mineral wealth. The salesman is seeking riches through the discovery of customers. In prospecting for accounts, the registered representative is like any other sales person. He must use every ethical means possible to contact people and make them into accounts.

Prospecting is one of his prime functions and has to be done constantly, combined, if possible, with some other necessary activity. To illustrate the ingenuity which must be employed, we cite the examples of W.S. and T.R.

W.S. read research reports on the subway. Invariably, he found someone looking at them over his shoulder. At first, W.S. was annoyed;

but he then reasoned that this might be a way to contact prospects. Now, when someone looks over his shoulder, he turns and asks if the on-looker would like to have W.S. send him his firm's market letter.

T.R. combined his daily constitutional with prospecting. T.R. walks to his office, a 10-block walk. On the way, he stops off and takes names from the directories in office buildings. He mails literature and then calls on them.

Prospecting Demands Enthusiasm

Prospecting for customers requires a positive, enthusiastic attitude. No prospector, whether he searches Alaska for gold, Africa for diamonds, or New York City for customers, can survive and succeed without having faith in his ability as well as endurance, without which there can be no hope. The job of building a clientele in the securities business is not an easy one. (Unless you are fortunate enough to have rich relatives and friends who trust your judgment!) But to the man who has even limited connections, it is a job that can be done—and when it is done, it provides tremendous rewards.

Business will not come to you automatically. You will have to go after it. Right now, stop and think: "How many people know that I'm seated behind this desk ready to do business?" The answer is "Not Many!" Your immediate family and your friends know that you are here, but of the thousands of people in your vicinity, not one of them is aware of your existence in the securities business. From your seat behind your desk, you must let as many people as possible, know that you are ready, willing, and able to service them. They will not come to you—you will have to go to them.

You Must Be a Moving Force

Nothing will happen unless you make it happen. You have to be the moving force needed to overcome the inertia of the potential investor. Most people are content to let things stay as they are, and do not seek out new ways of doing things. Ignorance may keep one who has not invested before from doing so now. No one will come beating at your door. It is you who will have to go knocking on doors. It is you who will have to go to the public.

The hard way can be the best way, as it was for E.R. He had collected a group of leads without telephone numbers. Rather than let them go to waste, he called on them in person. The reception given him was surprisingly cordial, and he was able to speak to the leads directly. He continued to call on leads in person and found the person-to-person approach an easier way to do business.

Let the Law of Averages Work for You

Prospecting and conversion of prospects into accounts is a matter of percentages: the more people you call upon, the more accounts you will get.

The first mathematical rule of this business is that it takes about 200 accounts to make a good living. Not all your accounts will be active. Probably 75 per cent of your income will come from 25 per cent of your accounts. Then there is always an attrition of accounts, which makes solicitation a constant necessity. However, before you get an account you need a prospect, and it usually takes four prospects to make one account. And before you get prospects you need suspects. You should count on needing 20 suspects to make one prospect. A suspect is someone you believe is a possible investor, a prospect is a suspect who has shown interest in investing, and an account is a prospect who has given you an order.

The progression looks like this:

20 suspects are needed to make one prospect,
4 prospects are needed to make one customer.

From the above tabulation you can see why 20 calls a day is minimum. This will afford you one prospect a day, or five a week, and five prospects a week should afford you one account a week. (Actually, your opening of new accounts will increase to a greater extent than indicated here because you will also be getting referrals from your accounts.)

Each Suspect Is Worth $2 to You

To proceed further with our mathematics, each account, on an average, will create $160 in gross commission. If each account is worth $160, then each prospect is worth $40 and each suspect is worth $2! All of this is by way of saying that each contact you make is worth $2 in gross commissions, and your earnings will grow in direct proportion to the number of calls you make.

Work Off Your Nervous Energy

J.C., as a new representative, found that sitting around the office all day "waiting for something to happen" was wearing on his nerves. He reasoned that if he just wanted to sit around, he should have become a storekeeper, who waited for people to come into his store. One of the leads the firm gave him was in a nearby office building. He walked over to see the man. The reception was cordial. After the meeting, he just couldn't see going back to sit around the office. He called, cold, on the office next door to the lead. He soon found that by making calls he worked off his nervous energy and was making money besides.

How Good Are Your Firm's Leads?

At this point you might ask "what about the leads from my firm?" As we cover leads more thoroughly later on, for now we only state that no firm can supply you with enough leads to keep you busy all day, and that in order to reach your goal of 20 calls, some of the leads will have to be your own. A lead is someone looking for assistance. Treat him with the proper respect, and he, in turn, will respect your approach to him. Each lead probably costs your firm between $5 and $10 apiece. Any item that expensive merits your sincerest and best attention. Don't treat the lead casually—he is a potential customer. Call him as soon as you receive the lead, introduce yourself, and ask him questions as outlined in Chapter 8.

Organize Your Prospecting

Prospecting, like all your other activities, must be systematized in order to be successful. You will require the following paraphernalia:

1. Pocket notebook.
2. Calling list form (see description of same on page 68).

3. Diary.
4. File box.
5. Alphabet filing cards of prospects.
6. Date filing cards.
7. Filing cards.

1. The pocket notebook is to be used as a repository for names gathered as suspects during the day. Set a goal of 20 a day. The sources of names will be taken up in Chapter 7.

2. The calling list form is your daily list of calls and the results. From this list will come your prospects and eventual customers. The form is to be filled out on the Saturday preceding your week's work. Fill in the name, address, phone, and occupation, leaving room for your remarks regarding the conversation. Place the week's supply on a clip board and make your calls every day.

3. The diary is your record of future calls. Presume that you called a suspect on June 4th. He asked you to call back on July 8th. In your diary, under July 8th, put him down for a call back. When you make up your call sheet for July 8th, you will be referring to your diary, and it will list his name as a call for that day. As you make your calls, your number of call backs will snowball, and you will find that getting 20 calls prepared for a day is too easy—you will be making even more calls than the minimum.

4. The file box is to be used to keep your prospect cards alphabetically. It is also to be used to schedule your call backs to prospects. The diary is essentially for the suspect list while the file box is for the prospect list.

5. Once a suspect has shown interest, he is now a pros-

pect. Prepare a 3 × 5 card on which you will put as much of the following information as you can gather about the prospect. This material is later to be used in your analysis of his needs:

```
Name: _____    Address: _____    Phone: _____
Business: _____    Address: _____    Phone: _____
Position: _____    Salary: _____    Married: _____
Owns or Rents: _____    Children (No. & Ages): _____
Cash Available: _____    Insurance: _____
Securities Held: _____
Investment Objectives: _____
```

The back of the card is for your record of calls and comments.

6. The prospect card is now placed in the date file for your call back. For example: On June 9th one of your suspects showed an interest in chemical stocks. You filled out the card, sent him reports on chemical stocks, and marked on the back of the card the date, material sent, and the call back date. You now place this card in the date file for June 12th. You may also have other cards waiting there for that day, so you now have several more calls added to that day's list. Each card will contain its own record of past results, and you will be able to resume your conversation where you left off. A sample prospect card with sample results will be found at the end of this chapter.

7. Your prospect will either become an account or will move to your inactive file, which will be kept by alphabet. He will now receive a maximum of one mail piece every

two weeks, and a minimum of one every three months. A periodic check-up of the inactive file will also turn up names to be called by phone from time to time.

The Rewards May Come Late or Soon, but They Come

The keeping of files as described above is necessary because there is no precise time limit from the first time a suspect is called to the time he becomes a customer. Among your 20 daily calls are some who will never become customers, some who will become customers in a month, some in three months, and some in a year or two years. There is no way of predetermining the time needed to convert a suspect into a customer. It is like cultivating a garden with seeds of an unknown gestation period. All you can do is add the water and provide the atmosphere needed for growth through judicious and periodic calls and mailing. Some plants will grow soon and some will come later, but the end result will be a well-grown garden from which you can reap your livelihood. As in any garden, some plants will wither and others must be weeded out; and like a good gardener, you will always be planting fresh seeds for replacement.

Again, you must keep about you the long-term point of view. If you are overly anxious, and try to rush the cultivation of your customers through pressure methods, you will kill them off. If you are lackadaisical, they will never grow for lack of nutrition.

Let the System Do the Work

By using the above system, you will have a method working for you which can only lead to success. The system is like your foreman; let it guide you. It is the framework within which you will build your clientele.

One Thing the System Cannot Do

However, there is one thing the system can't do: make you work. This force must come from within you.

The cyclical nature of the business may cause you to slow down at just those times when you should be working hardest. In a period of dull markets—and this period can extend for months!—you may become apathetic and say, "What's the use! No one I talk to buys or sells!" However, unless you maintain contacts in slow markets, you will have no one to talk to in busy markets, and subsequently will not do as much as you could do in the busy period. You will undoubtedly hear the expression, "This is a feast or famine business." It is only so to those who do not maintain a sustained work effort. In slow periods one has to look harder for business. Again, nothing will come to you unless you go out and get it. Instead of making 10 calls a day, you now need 20 calls a day. If stocks don't move, try bonds or mutual funds. Just sitting around the office waiting for something to happen is wishful thinking, and it is deleterious to your morale. No matter if business is slow, you keep working. Your spirits will pick up, and your new-found enthusiasm will help you to get accounts.

Think Positive

You must maintain a positive attitude at all times. You cannot let the vagaries of the stock market control your emotions. If the market goes down, don't go down emotionally with it; and if the market goes up, don't let your spirits rise out of proportion to the occasion. Unfortunately, your attitude is contagious to your customers, and you will not be doing them the best possible service if pessimism makes you lose sight of investment possibilities, or if undue optimism makes you take unnecessary risks. Investment opportunities exist in every kind of market. It is your function to be a cold, critical appraiser of these possibilities.

Don't Rather Be Right Than Registered

The new registered representative is so concerned with being right that he seeks someone else's opinion to lean on instead of sharpening his own critical faculties. Seek to develop your own independence of thought—of course, within the framework of your firm's research and guidance, and within all the rules and regulations necessary to the securities business.

You will make mistakes. Expect to make mistakes and do not feel badly about them. It is important to make mistakes. They are part of your learning process. Constantly review your activities in the light of the guidance afforded by this book. Ferret out your mistakes and correct them. For instance, if after what seemed like a successful interview you did not get an order, then think back to the interview and to the possible mistakes you may have made.

Mistakes Are One of Your Important Products

What did you say that was wrong; what did you neglect to say which should have been said? Mistakes help us sharpen our techniques. As your techniques improve, so will your list of customers.

Don't let mistakes get you down in spirits. Mistakes are necessary to help you do a better job the next time. Keep your generator going. Don't let mistakes slow you down—they are only one-time detours which you never take again.

CHAPTER 7

MANY ARE CALLED,
FEW ARE CHOSEN

IN NATURE, THE CREATION OF A LIVING THING
appears to be a rather haphazard process. The
oak tree drops hundreds of acorns before one
finally takes root and becomes a tree. The
salmon lays thousands of eggs, out of which very
few are actually fertilized. We could add count-
less other illustrations, and show their simi-
larity to the process of creating accounts; the
odds, however, are not quite so prodigious.
Since it is impossible to predetermine who will
and who will not be an account, we must first
gather our likely suspects. A suspect list has to
be prepared, and since the amount of names
needed is large, we must have available many
sources for our requirements. The list can be
prepared on legal-size pads. It should include

[74]

name, address, phone number, occupation, and any other vital information known to you.

First Look to the People You Know

The first list you make up should be that of the people you know. Set up the following categories and place the names you recall under the proper category. These will be the people you know from:

1. School.
2. Previous business.
3. Being related.
4. Societies and clubs.
5. Purchases I've made.
6. Services I use.
7. Being introduced by others.

You will soon have a list of at least 200 names, including former classmates, business associates, relatives, club members, storekeepers, doctors, gas station owners, plumbers, etc. This method we call the "FAR" system, for Friend, Acquaintance, and Relative, and it can help you to get "FAR." Next to each name, indicate the type of investment which you feel would be suitable for that person.

Put A.T.&T. to Work for You

Although telephone books may be hackneyed and overused as a source of names, they do have one important feature: the name and address is up-to-date. Anyone without experience in making a list is amazed at the number of people who change addresses in a short period of time. A list over six months old is almost worthless. Don't leave out the phone book. If culled carefully, many useful names can be drawn up. There are several suggested lists you can make. The first is comprised of women whose names are given in the phone book preceded by "Mrs." It is a reasonable assumption that these women are, in the main, widows. Widows are usually left money either outright or from insurance proceeds. A suggested way to approach them is with either a conservative, dividend-paying stock, or with mutual funds.

Studying the phone book further, we find individual men's names followed by a small "B." These names will give us a list of single proprietorship businessmen. The approach to this list is with the "businessman's risk" type of security, the semi-speculative stock. Another list of names can be made from women's names preceded by "Miss" or with no preceding title. These women are probably single and working. An approach to them can be made through M.I.P. or mutual fund plans.

The classified directory is useful for lists of professionals. It has a limited use for businessmen's names, because the businesses are listed by name and the proprietor's name is not given. The Street Address Directory can be used in large cities. By selecting a building in a better area of your city, you can provide yourself with the name and phone number of each person living in that building. This list will be heterogeneous in make-up, and will require a general method of approach rather than the specific illustrations given above. The average cost of renting the Street Directory is about $15 a month. It comes in a binder, and the Telephone Company keeps it up-to-date for you by adding new sheets to the book. It also will focus your prospecting in one area, and that will make it possible to make follow-up calls in person with a minimum of travel time.

A Rented List Can Help Put You in the Driver's Seat

Sooner or later you will ask yourself, "Should I rent a list of names?" The answer is "yes" if the list can meet certain qualifications. The list should be up-to-date, and the people neither too rich nor too poor. Don't rent a list of people advertised as having incomes of $25,000 or more. Invariably, the names are of individuals who are quite wealthy and impossible to reach; and if they are attainable, they will be too sophisticated for the new representative. However, seasoned representatives could use such a list to advantage. Don't buy stockholders lists. The price is usually quite high, and again, the choice of such lists is limited. If you can obtain a list of stockholders in a stock recently depressed, however, the investment could be worthwhile. The shareholders are usually glad to get your opinion on their problem stock. A preferable list is that of individuals who have recently made an expensive purchase; for instance, a list of individuals who spent $100 for a sidewalk snow cleaner, or who purchased a complete set of golf clubs. Chances are these people are well off enough to invest, but are not too rich to be unapproachable. Many of them may have just moved into their higher incomes and do not as yet have brokers. Such lists are available from list houses. The list house may have other names in categories that are suitable. Investigate the possibilities.

The cost of renting a list is about $25 per thousand names. However, you should analyze the list's possibilities very carefully before buying. Should you desire a special list, the list house will make it up for you at an additional cost of about another $10 per thousand.

Save $25—Make Your Own List!

Your daily newspaper is a constant source of names. There's the column on new appointments in business—who has been promoted in a firm or joined a company. We don't suggest contacting this man at once, but save the list for contact a month after he's settled down in his new job. Because the registered representative is trained to assist people in their financial planning, he can take notes of the obituary column. A widow with insurance money and no knowledge of investing lives off her principal and soon finds herself destitute. Statistics show that the widow left $25,000 uses it up in seven years. Again, save the list for a month and approach the widow with a sensible plan to receive dividends from quality securities; or, perhaps, a mutual fund. You will be performing a very important service to her. There is also the list of births. Eventually these children may go to college, but the parents have not given consideration to the tremendous expense they will have to face 18 years hence. Approach the list with some form of systematic investment.

Then there are names in the newspaper, under news stories, of those who have had a sudden windfall. Chances are the insurance agents will undertake to follow such a lead. Why not a stockbroker? Isn't his product also worthy of this individual's attention?

Most trades and professions have a directory. There are, for example, directories for the Jewelry Trades, Millinery Trades, Electrical Trades, Mechanical Engineers, Civil Engineers, Department Store Buyers, Variety Store Buyers, Teachers, and Certified Public Accountants. The list of such directories is very large, and each directory can be obtained from someone in the business or profession. It may also be obtained from the Trade Association or Professional Association. The benefit of using the trade directories is that they name the heads of the various firms. The possible approaches to lists from the directories are wide, ranging from information on the Keogh Bill for Self-employed Retirement Plans to stocks in companies allied to the profession: Electrical Stocks to Electrical Engineers, Department Store Stocks for the Store Buyers, etc.

Your Firm Can "Lead" the Way to Customers

The leads which your firm gives you also go on your list of suspects. They are primarily derived, in most firms, from newspaper advertising. In that same paper, the advertisements of several firms appear, and the person who answers your ad may have answered them all. He may be a minor, a coupon clipper, or someone serious about investing. You won't know which until you approach the lead. In the meanwhile, don't treat leads casually. Each lead costs your firm from $5 to $10.

The expense merits your sincerest attention to that

lead. Don't delay in contacting the person, and do so no later than two days after the information requested has been mailed to the lead. In some firms, the representatives will not follow the lead with a phone call, mainly because in that firm a false conception of the value of leads has been built up by the representatives. At some time in the past, in the firm which doesn't follow up leads with a phone call, some inept men called, got nowhere, and spread the story that leads are worthless. Other men, only too glad to have an opportunity not to work, accepted the myth, and ever since, in that firm, leads are not considered worthy of any effort. Of course, a great many leads *are* worthless, but a great many are worthwhile. There is no way to differentiate between the two until you make contact with the lead, because a lead is only as good as the salesman makes it. If every lead were to become a customer, there would be no need for salesmen.

Set an Endless Chain of Referrals to Work for You

Referrals are another source of suspects. We think of referrals as coming from existing accounts. This is not so. A person may refer you to many people, but never open an account with you! On the list of people you know, there may be an accountant who has maintained an account with another broker for many years. He does not wish to end a long standing relationship and will not give you his account, but will gladly refer others to you. Look in your list for people like this accountant who are in a position to refer names to you. There's your insurance agent. You might refer names for insurance, while he reciprocates with names for stocks. There are certain individuals to whom others look for guidance. These people exert an influence in their sphere of acquaintanceship. Such a person may be an executive in a company, an active member of a social group, or a well-established accountant. Be on the look-out for this type of person and cultivate him. The referrals he can give you will become accounts more readily because of his endorsement.

Constant searching for suspects is your only insurance against loss of business. Tomorrow's customers come from today's suspects. Once you become satisfied with your list of accounts and do not seek new ones, your business will only dwindle. Even the great corporations constantly seek out new markets and new customers. They know that they cannot stop growing, for the alternative to growth is stagnation.

Keep Up Your Most Wanted List of Suspects

Keep a notebook with you at all times in which to collect names of suspects. At every opportunity gather names from whatever source available to you, from directories in the Public Library to names supplied by friends and relatives. Upon contacting a person who is not responsive, ask him if he knows of someone who *is* interested in investing. People are quite willing to do small favors, and you will soon find that your suspect-collecting activities will produce an endless chain of names.

If a prospect does not open an account, don't relegate him to the inactive file without first asking if he knows the name of one person who can use your services. If you have served him courteously and efficiently, he may very well give you the name of someone. In asking for referrals, always ask for the name of one person. Never say, "Do you know any others who might be interested?" The prospect envisions you calling on all his friends and thereby causing him to lose their friendship. But, if you ask for just one name, he can give you that with impunity. Of course, after you have received one name, you can then ask, "Can you think of one more name?" You will probably come away with two referrals.

CHAPTER 8

THE APPROACH, OR, QUALIFYING THE PROSPECT

HAVING PREPARED A LIST OF SUSPECTS, WE NEED to find a means of converting them into qualified prospects. The approach can be made by mail, by phone, or by a combination of both. Sending out mailings to suspect lists which call for a return card may give you names which are not necessarily prospects. A qualified prospect is one who has evinced a definite interest in investing. One who returns a reply card may have done so out of interest or out of casual curiosity. Mailings, therefore, are a means of preparing a better suspect list, but mailings do not do the job of converting "suspects" to prospects. To make prospects of "suspects," the following methods are recommended:

1. Mail out three-way reply cards, or a letter with a reply card offering literature. (Although the three-way reply cards are cheaper

[83]

to mail, the quality of the response is lower.) Upon receipt of the reply, send out the literature immediately and follow up with a phone call in no later than three days.

2. Mail out a specific piece of literature and call one day later with a prepared talk designed to arouse interest.

You will have the problem of preparing letters to go with the aforementioned material. Don't try to write a selling letter. It is sure to break the regulations regarding written presentations. If possible, have the letter written by your firm's advertising agency. They are not only cognizant of the rules, but can prepare effective letters. If you write the letter yourself, have it checked by a partner, and if questions remain about the letter being within regulations, you may submit it to the New York Stock Exchange and/or the N.A.S.D. for any required changes.

Sample Bag of Approaches

SAMPLE APPROACH 1: Having decided to use the list of widows which we drew from the phone book, we now need mailing matter. Looking over the mailing material that is available, we have decided that a proper approach would be the booklet, *Investment Facts*. Because we are dealing with a specific group with a specific problem, we wish to prepare a letter to appeal to that group and that problem. It is our assumption that widows would be interested in income as well as long-term growth as a hedge against inflation. Our letter is as follows:

Do you need more income
to meet Rising Living Costs?

The rising costs in food, rent and clothing have caused
many women like yourself to look into quality com-

mon stocks with long records of dividend payments. Some of these stocks have paid dividends for the past thirty years or more. The booklet **Investment Facts,** contains a list of these long-term dividend-paying stocks with their current rates of return. You are invited to receive one free with no obligation on your part. Just return the enclosed card and we will be pleased to send you a copy.

SAMPLE APPROACH 2: Having decided to use the list of businessmen we gathered from the phone book, we decide to offer a copy of "How to Read a Financial Statement," as well as our firm's research report. Our covering letter is as follows:

If You Have Ever Invested
or Have Considered Investing . . .

You are sure to find the New York Stock Exchange pamphlet **How to Read a Financial Statement** of special interest in helping you to investigate before you invest. The enclosed card is for your convenience in ordering a copy free of charge. We will also include our latest Research Department Report. There is no obligation.

SAMPLE APPROACH 3: Your firm has prepared a report on Insurance Company Stocks. You use this opportunity to approach insurance agents and brokers. You prepare a letter as follows:

How does the Insurance Company
you represent rate?

Our report on the Insurance Industry may give you a new outlook on your industry and on your own investments. To receive your copy of this report, kindly fill in below and return in the enclosed envelope.

Please send a copy of your Insurance Industry Report.

Name _____   Address _____

Introduce Yourself

With a little imagination you can adapt your lists and the available promotional materials into effective sales campaigns. But do not expect miracles. A well-written letter, a handsome brochure, and a firm's good name are not sufficent to produce sales. Don't expect the mailman to do your selling for you. Mailings are used only as a means of opening a door for you. They only provide the initial contact, after which you must broaden out and expand your relationship with the prospect, in order to make him a customer.

Be Prepared

Do not establish an approach with the fixed idea that the item used for the approach will be the one purchased. In your approach to the widows, you used the theme of "Dividends," but do not carry with you the preconceived notion that every widow will settle for dividends. For example, you may very well come across some rich widows who can afford to speculate, and know the risks involved.

As a result of an M.I.P. campaign you may get replies from 60-year-olds who have no need of M.I.P. They do, however, have an interest in investing, and will reply, hoping to get some investment information. Don't be surprised when this happens. It does give you an opportunity to talk about out-right investment for income. Your approach can lead to any possibility. Do not assume that your respondents know precisely to what they are replying. You may have an incident similar to this one happen to you:

G.G., on an M.I.P. mailing, established contact with: (a) a man 70 years old who owned real estate holding company stocks; (b) a man, age 62, who invested in quality stocks for long-term; (c) an active trader who wanted to do something for his children; and (d) a new investor with $5,000 available for investment.

A More Dynamic Approach

Although a return of 1 percent to 2 percent is to be expected from a mail campaign, the effectiveness can be increased if each recipient of a letter is also called. The total response can be increased up to 10% if a phone call follow-up is used. A great many suspects are interested, but just don't take the time or make the effort to reply. You can combine your mailing list with your list of daily calls. Sending a mail piece with a follow-up phone call is not a technique unique to the securities business. It has been used in other lines as well, and always increases the percentage of interested suspects.

The telephone call is not to be made haphazardly. You must know precisely what you are going to say. You can write out your talk and keep it in front of you when you call. Make sure to prepare the wording for a spoken presentation differently from a written presentation. We do not speak as we write. It is important to keep the informality of the spoken word in the write-up.

Practice your prepared talk on someone close to you, and ask his opinion as to whether it rings true. If you do not wish to write out a talk, practice one until you have it down pat.

In following up your mail campaign to the widows, you can use a phone call with this sample presentation:

> Good Evening, is this Mrs. Brown?
>
> Mrs. Brown, my name is Mr. _____ of _____; we are stockbrokers. The other day we sent you a letter about stocks which pay dividends. In the letter we offered to send you a booklet telling all about dividend-paying stocks. Would you like to have us send you a copy?

Upon receiving approval to send the material, do so with a covering letter similar to the following:

> Dear _____:
>
> We are pleased to enclose a copy of _____. Although this informative booklet will be of help to you, there may be questions you wish answered. I will take the liberty of calling you to ask if I may be of assistance.
>
> Yours truly,

No later than three days after the literature is mailed, call the suspect.

The phone call is to be used for fact-finding and no attempt should be made to sell. You should be firm, courteous, and even casual, but have a definite purpose to the conversation.

Ask Questions in Depth

The phone call is to provide you with enough information to determine if the suspect can be converted to a prospect. A sample phone call is given below to serve you as a guide. Do not expect the call to follow a set pattern. You will need versatility in your conversation. Don't let the other party lead you away from the purpose of your call. Your aim is to find out information about the suspect, and to give him enough information about investing for him to become a prospect:

"Good Evening, Mr. _____, this is _____ of _____. A few days ago I sent you information about investing. Did you find it of interest to you?"

If the answer is yes, proceed to determine why it was of interest and how it will meet his investment need.

If the answer is no, ask him why he replied and what type investment he was seeking. Find out for what purpose he should invest. Ask questions:

"What do you do for a living?
How old are you?
How old are your children?
Do you own stocks?
If you were to invest what would you want: dividends? profits? long-term growth?
Do you have any surplus money for investment?"

Do not ask questions in a cold factual manner. Upon receiving a reply to a question, comment upon the answer to show that you are aware of his problems. For example, having received a reply that he is foreman in a plant, you might comment about the responsibility of his job; also ask him if he is covered by a pension plan. If he owns stocks, ask for the list for analysis purposes. If he has never invested, ask why he has not. Ask this to find out if he has fear, prejudice, or lack of understanding about investing. Determine his attitudes towards investing. Does he look upon investing with the mistaken motion that it is a means for getting rich quickly? Does he believe the broker's function is to provide him with "tips"? Is he aware of the difference between speculation and investment? Has he, in the past, purchased stocks on which he had a loss? Has this experience made him turn against investing? Is he seeking to make up for his losses? Is he cautious? Is he imprudent and taking risks he cannot afford? What does he want investments to accomplish for him? Does his wife agree with him about undertaking an investment program?

You, in turn, inform him of the possible risks and possible rewards of investing. Advise him that:

1. There is no perfect investment.
2. The choice of the proper investment depends on his requirements.
3. You are available to provide him with information about investing which he can use as a basis to make his decisions.
4. Although possibilities of loss exist, the careful selection of securities and your supervision of his holdings may help him achieve his investment objectives.

5. Before investing, he should have savings and life insurance.
6. If he has invested, you can review his holdings at no cost.
7. He should not act on tips and rumors.
8. Also, you may want to tell him that the past history of your firm and/or yourself may be of benefit to him.
9. There is a difference between growth stocks and dividend-paying stocks.
10. There is an importance to him of capital gains, if he is in a high tax bracket.

From this exchange of information, determine whether or not the individual is a prospective investor, and if so, for what type investment.

Some Ideas for the New Representative

The new representative finds that he has too much time. Not having enough customers, he may sit around the office watching the ticker tape and do little to develop customers. During office hours, a prospecting campaign can be accomplished through the use of mail with a follow-up phone call. Many campaigns can be devised and built around the literature available.

Select 10 names of business or professional men from the phone book. List the names, addresses, occupations, and phone numbers on a legal pad. Leave a margin to the right for comments. Place the date of mailings at the top of the page, and also the date for a call back, which should be two business days later.

You may use your firm's market letter with an accompanying letter. The letter can be multigraphed so that only the suspect's name has to be typed in. The letter may read as follows:

Mr. John Grove
151 Broadway
New York, New York

Dear Mr. Grove:

Enclosed please find a complimentary copy of our firm's Market Letter. We are sending you this report in order to acquaint you with only one of the many services which we afford investors.

I will take the liberty of calling you in a few days to ask if we may be of assistance to you.

Sincerely yours,

Two days later you will call Mr. Grove. Keep in front of you a prepared speech. The prepared speech serves two purposes: (a) by focusing your attention on the written words, your tension will be lessened; and (b) by being prepared you will come across to Mr. Grove with clearness and forcefulness. The prepared speech should approximate your own speech patterns. A sample follows:

Mr. Grove, this is _____ of _____, a member firm of the New York Stock Exchange. Yesterday you received a copy of our firm's Market Letter. I'm calling to ask you if you wish to receive the next four copies at no obligation.

If the answer is "no," go on to the next call. If the

answer is "yes," say "Are there any stocks in which you have a special interest so that I may include reports on them?" Wait for an answer, and then ask him what stocks he now holds. Upon receiving this information, you now have a good suspect. He is still not a prospect, but your chance of converting him has improved.

Another sample campaign is as follows:

Obtain a list of housewives with young children; mail to them a prospectus and past record of a mutual fund plan, together with a brochure on the cost of a college education. The covering letter can read:

Dear Mrs. _____:

The cost of sending one child to college is $8,000. Costs are expected to increase in the years to come. Won't it be sensible to help meet this cost by a sound plan of investment?

Enclosed is information on such a plan, including the past record and the possible risks. You will notice that large sums of money are not needed.

I will call you in a few days to ask if I may be of any further assistance.

Sincerely yours,

On the call back, have your prepared speech before you; it could read like this:

This is _____ of _____, securities dealers. A few days ago we sent you information on a plan to send your child to college. I'd like to ask one question. Are you doing anything about your child's education now?

Wait for answer. If the answer is "no," say "Mrs.

_____, don't you think you should have a definite plan to send your child to college?"

If the answer is "no," ask why. If "yes," ask for an appointment. "Can I see you Tuesday at 8 P.M. or Wednesday at 7 P.M., whichever is more convenient for you?"

The woman may very well say that her husband must discuss the matter with you. Ask her to give the literature to her husband and say that you will call him. Ask her for a convenient time to reach her husband.

When you call the husband, start the conversation by saying, "Mr. _____, your wife suggested I call you." Repeat the prepared speech previously given to the wife.

Send out the brochure, *Investment Facts*, with a covering letter similar to the following:

> As members of the New York Stock Exchange, one of our services, offered with no obligation, is to assist investors in the selection of those securities suitable to their investment requirements. You may have been considering investing and need advice in your selection, or you may own securities on which you now require an opinion.
>
> The enclosed booklet, **Investment Facts**, may be of interest to you in formulating an opinion. I will take the liberty of calling you to ask if our many years of experience may be placed at your disposal.
>
> Sincerely yours,

Have your prepared speech read:

"This is Mr. _____ of _____, a member firm of the New York Stock Exchange. In my recent letter to you, I offered our services to help you select or to analyze a stock. Do you have a problem stock, one on which you would like an opinion? If so what stock is it?"

If the answer is "no," ask if he would like to be placed on your mailing list for Market Letters.

Does It Really Pay to Prospect?

After reading the previous campaign you may very well be saying, "This is all very well, but I still don't see how any of these people will turn into customers."

Doing the things recommended in the preceding pages is, of course, not going to create customers; it will only create prospects. It is now up to you to determine what type of investment each of the individuals might use. Here we come to the heart of the registered representative's problem. The prospect usually has one idea of what he should purchase—or perhaps no idea. It is up to the registered representative to analyze the prospect's needs and point them out to him. Do so in a clear, explicit manner. If you do not present yourself in a direct and bold manner, the prospect will not respect you.

Some say that our business has, over the years, been plagued by mediocrity. If this has been true, a new wind is blowing through our ranks today, driving out the incompetent and mediocre, and leaving room only for the well-trained. We are called upon each day to make selections for customers. We must select that which is directly suitable, or else face loss of business, prestige, and earnings. You will find, unfortunately, that some people may look upon the stock market as a great gambling hall. If some use it as such, it should only be those who can afford losses. To most it should be a means of investing and sharing in the growth and earnings of American industry. Explain the difference between investing and speculating. Ask Mr. Jones if he can afford to lose money, if he expresses a wish to speculate. Advise Mr. Smith that his ideas on long-term investment are sound—that quality stocks may fluctuate, but if they do decline, sooner or later they may come back to the same or even higher prices.

Above all, be truthful to yourself and your customer. People are not fools; they can be fooled once, but once fooled can never be recovered as customers. You must ask many, many questions before you make a recommendation. Many investors, especially the business man or professional man, will take the attitude that he knows as much as, or more than, you. This is wrong; do not let him adopt this superior attitude. It is as though when it comes to his money, no one can advise him but himself. He looks upon himself as being his best guide, for since he has been successful in his business or profession, he feels capable of making all his own decisions. If you let him maintain that attitude, he will have no respect for you. You must be forceful and dynamic, and be willing and capable to challenge his opinions. The big accounts go to the man who shows the confidence born of his training and experience. You must make decisions and recommendations without equivocation. No one respects a vacillator, but everyone respects a person of action and decision. If you have researched a selection and believe it to be good, say so. Say to him, "Mr. Investor, I recommend XYZ corporation because . . ."

Stick to your reasons and to your evaluation. Don't

retreat. "Mr. Investor" will only have respect for you if you are firm and if you are right! Search very carefully before making a recommendation. Do not be held back by a fear of making mistakes; but do recognize your mistakes and don't be blinded by over-confidence. By admitting your mistakes, your forthrightness may save the day. People will like you if you have a positive attitude. Speak firmly and with knowledge. You will get customers. People look for leadership; *be* that leader. Study, learn to know of what you speak, and speak affirmatively. The business will follow.

This same positive, affirmative attitude must be carried out in the approach. No one will answer questions addressed to him by an incompetent. Your only hope of doing business with someone is to have him divulge enough about himself for you to analyze his needs. If you ask questions in an apologetic or weak manner, you will not be answered. Maintain a dignified attitude at all times. If the prospect asks you why you are asking so many questions, answer him truthfully—you can only advise him if you know him, and unless he will answer your questions, you cannot help him.

Above all, maintain your air of dignity. You are in this business to serve people, but not based on *their* opinions and demands. You must filter their ideas through your *own* mind in order to test their validity. You are the ultimate judge of what is suitable for the customer. You lead, and the prospect follows. If he refuses to take your advice, and buys those securities not meant for him, you at least have done your duty, and you cannot be recriminated against.

The approach works two ways. Just as you are qualifying the prospect, he is qualifying your abilities. If you give sound advice, suited to the investor's requirements, you will meet the "qualification test."

CHAPTER 9

THE INTERVIEW

FOR OUR PURPOSE, THE INTERVIEW IS THE MEANS of obtaining information about the prospect which will enable us to serve his investment needs properly. We ordinarily tend to think of an interview as a face-to-face affair, with one party asking well-chosen questions and the other party giving the sought-for reply. But all our interviews will not be held face-to-face.

Most of our interviews—or information-gathering—will be obtained in one or more phone conversations.

Know Your Customer

Knowledge of one's customer is made mandatory by Rule 405 of the New York Stock Exchange and the Rules of Fair Practice of the N.A.S.D. This knowledge is not to be confined only to the person's financial ability to meet his commitments, but also extends to his investment needs and requirements. It is certainly wrong to buy securities for an account only to find that he hasn't the means to pay. It is also wrong not to know your customer well enough to be aware that he might back out on an exchange contract if it turned against him before settlement date. It is equally wrong to analyze your customer's needs and to fail to give advice appropriate to his individual financial requirements.

The question of providing proper advice is not simply a matter of being right if the stocks recommended do go up, and being wrong if the stocks recommended go down. Securities are graded by quality, and the research studies available to any representative makes proper selection a not too difficult problem. Too often, the representative lets the customer's desires rather than his needs be his guide. The customer usually doesn't know enough about investing to make his own decisions. How often does the person of limited means try speculation as a means of acquiring wealth, while he cannot afford to lose the little he has? How often has the one who should be a long-term investor tried to take a short cut via the most volatile stocks? It is the representative's duty to point out the customer's needs as opposed to his wants. If the customer still insists on speculating when you have advised him not to, or if he wants to buy the security inferior in quality to the one you recommended, you may fulfill his wishes, but if your firm has not instituted the procedure of marking orders "solicited" or "unsolicited," you should make a brief memo of the conversation, time-stamp it in your order room, and keep it on file. If the purchase declines, you may have protected yourself and your firm against any complaint.

The interview, therefore, is more than a means of inquiring about the investor's needs; it is also a means of inquiring about his abilities to meet his commitments. Neither is the interview a one-sided affair. Just as you are interviewing the customer, he, in a sense, is interviewing you to determine whether you are the broker for him.

Each interview must be planned in advance. You must have as much knowledge of the prospect as you can obtain before calling on him. You must have a series of objectives to be obtained from the interview. The objectives are, in order of importance:

1. To get an order.
2. Get a date for call back.
3. Make recommendations.
4. Get family and job data.
5. Get list of holdings.
6. Get his reasons for investing.
7. Advise how you and your firm can help him.
8. Keep on mailing list for call back at indefinite date.

Although the objectives are listed by importance, you will try to accomplish them in ascending order, with #8 your minimum accomplishment and #1 your maximum accomplishment.

Control That Interview

Control of the interview must be in your hands. Here is an example of the controlled interview:

J.T. has had many years of experience as a representative. He was referred to a doctor in Queens, New York, as a possible account. He was told that the doctor sought advice from every source and kept his desk loaded with research reports from all over. Before J.T. called for an appointment, he thought out a plan for the interview. He believed that he had hit upon the right approach, and made an appointment. When he came to the doctor's office, the desk was piled high with reports; more than any one man, let alone a busy doctor, could ever hope to read. The doctor said to J.T., "Put your stuff down here and I'll read it when I get a chance." J.T. looked the doctor squarely in the eye and said, "I didn't come here to drop off a few pieces of paper; I came here to talk about you." And he pointed his finger at the doctor to emphasize his words. "First let's get rid of all this junk." J.T. picked all the reports off the desk and dumped them into the waste paper basket. He then sat down, and the doctor talked openly and gladly. J.T. had taken control of the interview. The doctor respected his mastery of the situation and became a substantial account.

Control of the interview can only come by adhering to the schedule of minimum and maximum objectives, and asking the questions which will lead to the attainment of the objectives. You are not conducting the interview to hold a casual conversation. The prospect will have no respect for a man who calls him up and wastes his time with a great deal of pointless chatter. When you talk to someone it has to be for a purpose, and you must make clear who you are and the reason for your call.

Decisions, Decisions, Decisions!

The normal reaction of the prospect is to think of reasons why he should not make any decisions. If I told you that a life insurance salesman were going to call on you tonight, your immediate reaction would be to find all the reasons why you do not need life insurance. When you call the prospect and state your business, his immediate reaction is defensive—he musters all the reasons why he shouldn't do anything. You will be called upon to show the reasons why he *should* invest, if he can. You will be engaged in a sort of fencing match, with the prospect either "selling" you that he shouldn't invest, or you "selling" him that he should invest. (Of course, the word "sell" is used advisedly above, and only in the sense that your arguments are valid as well as convincing.)

Set the Stage

Try to choose an hour for the interview that affords the prospect plenty of time. Don't have the prospect rush off because you called at some inopportune hour, and do not make an appointment to see him prior to an important meeting on his part. Evening calls to the home are the best means of having the time for a satisfactory interview. Should you have any reason to believe that the wife will exert influence on the decisions (and you should have reason to believe this very often), make an appointment to see both at their home. You may find the wife more conservative than the husband, and you will have the problem of choosing securities to meet their needs without hurting the husband's ego or moving the wife into a pique.

Never argue with the customer. The man may be as wrong as can be, and yet you say, "You may be right, but . . ." and give your reasons for believing him wrong.

The interview will be carried out with someone who has evinced some interest in your product. As yet, you don't know what type security suits him, and you will make no quick decisions. Very often, the prospect will set traps for you. He will lead you on by asking a great many questions about different securities, and then ask, "Which one shall I buy?" Your only answer can be "I don't know you well enough yet to advise you." If you name a security, he will cut the conversation short because of your eagerness to get an order without finding out his needs.

As you talk to the prospect, take notes on the card you have prepared for him. Ask the questions which will provide you with the information asked for. Don't ask the questions in a mechanical manner. People don't like to feel as though they are being interrogated. Your most important question will be the simple three-letter one, "Why?" By proper questioning, you can help people to see themselves. Don't wait to use "Why?" by accident. Such was the case of K.B., a registered representative for nearly a year, who stumbled across the technique of using "Why?" inadvertently. While conversing with a prospect, a retired middle-aged man, the man told him that he had recently bought a very volatile stock. K.B., without thinking, said "Why?" The idea seemed so preposterous that he fairly shouted it into the telephone. The man, sensing K.B.'s sincerity, said apologetically, "I guess I was just stupid." K.B.'s question helped the man see his actions in their proper perspectives.

If the prospect balks at answering your questions, the reason usually is that you have not as yet earned his confidence. Very often, prefacing your queries by saying that the only way you can be of proper service to the prospect is by asking him some personal questions may be sufficient to warrant his replying.

Be Casual in Opening the Interview

You may start the interview by first telling the prospect something about yourself and your firm. "Mr. Green, my name is _____ of _____, a member of the New York Stock Exchange. We have been helping investors since 1926, and the reason for my call is to ask if I can be of service to you. You inquired about Utility Securities. May I ask what your reason is for being interested in Utilities?"

The prospect can offer three possible replies:

      1. I was just curious.
      2. I own some utilities.
      3. I was considering them.

Your replies are as follows:

To #1: I'm glad you are curious, because it is important to investigate carefully before you invest. Do you have a special reason for investing—are you looking primarily for possible growth or primarily for dividends?

To #2: Which utilities do you own? Why did you select utilities?

To #3: Why are you considering utilities? What feature are you looking for in an investment—stability, possible growth, or dividends?

The above queries will lead to your obtaining his investment objectives. You then continue:

Mr. Green, you just told me that you are looking for dividends. Do you need the extra dividends to help you live, or is your salary sufficient to meet your expenses?

Or,

Mr. Green, you just told me you want growth of capital. How old are you? Is your income sufficient for you not to need dividends?

Or,

Mr. Green, you just told me that you want to make money fast. Can you afford to speculate? There's also the chance of loss there, you know.

The above questions help to pinpoint in his mind what his objectives should be.

Some prospects won't talk, but here's a technique which can help make them do so:

While on a call made by appointment, the writer, after some informal talk, was asking the prospect many questions, which the prospect decided not to reply to, and he kept his mouth shut. The writer kept throwing questions hoping to get a response, but the prospect just said nothing! The writer then asked one more question, slowly and deliberately. And then he sat back and shut up too. It then became a contest as to who would speak first. The prospect did answer the question, and then a few more. In fact, he became quite talkative. He never became an account, however, but the writer learned a lesson. There is a time in the interview to just shut up and let the prospect do some thinking. Some people only answer after due deliberation.

Be a Semanticist

Although you, trained in the securities business, will know the meaning of such words as *growth, dividends, income,* and *speculate,* your prospect may not fully understand their meaning. Do not assume knowledge of investing and investments on the prospect's part. Be sure to make your meaning clear, without in any way showing condescension.

In order to help define his objectives, you may be called upon to explain the meanings of the above words in the course of your conversation. Many intelligent people are simply uninformed about investing, as this case bears out:

Following up a Mutual Fund lead, B.H. found out that the prospect, a successful dentist, wished to invest towards his son's education. He decided on a high dividend-paying Mutual Fund in order that the dividends could compound and thereby increase his capital. B.H. pointed out that growth type securities were what he really needed.

Instead of paying out dividends on which he would have to pay taxes, they reinvest their earnings internally, and compound their growth in that fashion. The prospect was appreciative of B.H.'s knowledge and assistance. He became a good source for referrals.

Mr. Green has just said that he wants to speculate. You in turn say to Mr. Green:

> Mr. Green, I'm sure you know that speculating means taking high risks. I wouldn't feel comfortable letting you speculate unless I were sure you could afford to take risks where you may lose money. Of course, there's always the opportunity for profits, but let's go into this with our eyes open. Will you have set aside other money besides what you'll place in stocks? In other words, I'd like to make sure that you are not putting your last penny into speculations.

Mr. Green may very well say that he's a mature man who knows what he is doing, and may even think you are a bit naive; however, he will admire your sincerity in pointing out the risks of investing as well as the possible rewards.

No one can complain of your directness and of your asking incisive questions if they are asked only for that person's best interests.

Mr. Green might have chosen income as his objective, and decided that a 7 percent return would be to his liking. You will have to explain to Mr. Green that a high return may mean an abnormal risk; also be sure he knows the relationship between yield and safety of principal.

Having defined the objectives, and having the prospect understand the meaning of his objectives, you continue to ask more questions concerning his financial background. You still have to get to know him better, because you cannot simply accept his opinion as to what his financial goal should be.

The next information to acquire is data on job and family. Ask such questions as:

What do you do for a living?
How old are you?
Do you earn over $10,000 or under?
What income tax bracket are you in?
How old are you?
Do you have money in the bank and do you have life
insurance?

If he has his own business, get information about the type of business and the number of employees.

If he is in a high tax bracket, get the exact amount of the income tax bracket.

The answers to your questions will come more easily as you proceed. Remember, too, that we live in an age of questionnaires, and people are used to giving information about themselves.

Become "Simpatico"

We do not wish to give the impression that one should just methodically ask a series of questions. The representative should intersperse a comment after each reply, before proceeding with the next question. For example, having been given a boy's age as 10 he might say, "That's the age when they're the most fun and the most trouble." If the representative has children, he can say that he, too, has a child and mention his age. By showing the prospect that he is in a similar position, he helps build the rapport necessary for doing business together. When told the kind of business the prospect is in, ask about present business conditions. In short, ask about those things which everyone likes to talk about: himself, his job, his children, and his hopes for the future. *Listen well.* Speaking well is only half your job. Equally important is listening with understanding and patience. Talk about yourself only to the extent that it is needed to form a cordial relationship. Don't air any of your personal troubles or problems. No one likes to do business in securities with someone who has problems; there is the hidden fear that the problems will keep him from doing his job properly. People are often more careful about their money than their health. A man may go without a physical check-up for five years, but when he invests, he can't be too cautious.

To help build a personal relationship, L.M., now a partner in a member firm, would read up on a particular industry, such as machinery, woolens, etc., and then go call on businessmen in that industry. His knowledge of their business astonished them, and they were pleased to do business with so knowledgeable a broker.

Analyze Prospects as Well as Securities

After having acquired all this information, if you believe your knowledge of his needs and your choice of recommendations are proper, you may proceed to the presentation immediately, and try to open an account. However, only the more experienced representative can do this, and for the newer man, we suggest that he collect his notes and make a date for a call back in order to make the presentation. He will use that intervening time for analysis and the gathering of suitable recommendations.

The representative will have before him a card which will list all of the following information: name, address, age, marital status, children, position, income, securities held, investment objectives, and notes. From this information, he will analyze the prospect's needs. Let us look at sample cards as a lesson in proper analysis.

Sample Prospects

PROSPECT #1   **How Obtained:** M.I.P. Mailing

Name: Fred Benson   **Address:** 716 Hill Ave., San Francisco, Calif.   **Phone:** YO 4-6008

Business: Has own business—lumber yard   **Address:** 54 Grant, San Francisco, Calif.   **Phone:** YO 4-6129

Age: 43   **Children:** 2— Boy 9 and Girl 7

Income: (about) $15,000   **Cash:** $6,000

Holds: All very speculative issues. All down 50% or more. **Objectives:** Long-term growth. **Notes:** Has considered investing a gamble; pick the right stock and win. Has learned a lesson but is extremely cautious about where he will invest. Seems to realize that he needs investments, but has been "burned." **Analysis:** Build Benson's confidence in investing. Point out difference between speculation and investment. Suggest high-quality stocks. Suggested pieces to mail to him before calling back, are **Richest Man in Babylon; Investor's Primer,** No's 1 & 2. Select four or five quality issues for long-term growth potential. Benson can also use an investment plan to accumulate college funds for his children. (Hold in abeyance until account is established.) Benson can use a self-retirement plan in his business (also hold for later).

PROSPECT #2   **How Obtained:** House lead

Name: Blanche Morgan **Address:** 47 Crescent St., Los Angeles, Calif. **Phone:** LO 9-1354

Business: Copywriter, Trent Agency **Address:** 358 Market St., Los Angeles, Calif. **Phone:** MO 3-2468

Age: 29 **Single**

Income: $8,000 **Cash:** $2,000

Holdings: None

Notes: Knows nothing about investing. Has heard of people in the office who have made money in the market. Wishes to commit $1000 to speculation. Evidently misguided. **Analysis:** Miss Morgan needs some basic investment education. Send **Does It Make Sense for Me to Buy Stocks.** Advise her against speculation and suggest a sound dividend-paying stock or Mutual Fund. Can also use an investment plan to build capital.

From the above example, we can see the importance of gathering the facts and analyzing the situation. In the case of Benson, there was the opportunity for three sales: securities for himself, an investment plan for his children, and a retirement plan for his business. In the instance of

Miss Morgan, there were two possible sales: securities for cash, and an investment plan. Literature was mailed to each prospect in keeping with their investment needs and as a means of keeping the representative in the forefront of their minds.

Based upon your analysis, you will gather all the written material needed for the presentation. You may require current reports and evaluations of certain securities. Obtain same from your Research Department, and have a comprehensive report typed out and addressed to the prospect. Do not mail the report. If possible, deliver it in person for a face-to-face meeting. Remember: It is very easy to say "no" to a voice on the telephone; it is not so easy to say "no" to someone who has taken the effort to come to your home or office.

Psychology Also Helps

Your analysis must also include your evaluation of the emotional factors which will have to be overcome in making the "sale." Benson, we learned, had bought some speculative stocks on which he had lost money. He will be afraid of taking further losses. Miss Morgan looks upon stocks as a gambling vehicle. She has no proper perspective about the securities market. Upon being advised that she may also lose money in speculations, she may decide not to invest and you may not get an order. However, it would be better to lose the order than to have a disgruntled customer.

In your analysis you must be as dispassionate as possible. In no way should possible commissions influence or alter your thinking. First in your mind must be the benefit of the prospect.

Use the Guidance of Your Superiors

In your early months as a representative, it would be best for you to review your analysis with a partner or manager to make sure that your thinking is correct. What is right for the customer is right for you. Proper analysis will help to keep down the turnover in your accounts. It is the first stage in keeping customers.

Your analysis will also include the prospect's idea of his objectives. You will have to educate the prospect away from any wrong opinions he may have as to his objectives. One common form of misguided opinion was met and solved by V.G.

V.G.'s prospect was a 42-year-old professional man earning $20,000 a year. Having come from a poor family, he could only see stocks for their dividends. To him, dividends were tangible proof that his holdings were doing something. V.G., from the list of holdings, made up a schedule of the dividends received the past year, and in red pencil gave the amount which the Government took in taxes on those dividends. V.G. made up another schedule of companies for growth, and listed the retained earnings per share (possible dividend money retained in the business) on which the customer paid no taxes. V.G.'s demonstration proved the point. The prospect changed his opinion about his objective.

During the interview, since you are being analyzed by

the prospect, you must maintain your air of the well-trained registered representative. Do not: (a) get overly familiar, (b) tell jokes in bad taste, (c) boast about your past record unless you can prove it, or (d) use a wrong choice of words. Be on the alert for the prospect to test you. Just as you will ask questions, he will ask questions. Keep a record of your answers so that you do not cross yourself. He may, for instance, ask your opinion about an issue on which his mind has already been made up. He wants to determine if your thinking coincides with his, and if it does not, your reasons for not thinking the way he does must be valid. You must be prepared to back up your opinions with good arguments. Don't offer an opinion if you don't know. It is worse to be caught making believe you know, than not to know. You can always say you'd rather not offer a quick opinion without reviewing, let us say, the present tobacco situation with its day-to-day changes. Every part of you is being analyzed both subconsciously and consciously by the prospect. People form decisions about others from surface qualities as well as those qualities which can only be determined after having known the person for a while. Make sure your surface qualities show you off to best advantage—your dress, speech, tone of voice, use of language, cheerfulness, and enthusiasm are your surface qualities which offer the initial attractions.

Women know the importance of surface qualities. They are always careful to cultivate those mannerisms of dress and deportment which make them most attractive.

The representative must adopt the same attitudes toward showing himself off in the best manner possible. As for the deeper qualities, such as your analytical ability and your capability in coming up with suitable suggestions, these will come with practice. Again, don't worry about making mistakes. In the beginning, these are important to your learning process. No person and no book can teach you all there is to know. We can only offer guidance. The training camp can prepare you for combat, but it is only under fire that you can prove yourself. It is one thing to have an instructor simulate an interview and play the part of a man with $100,000 to invest. It is still another thing to be in the presence of a man with $100,000 to invest, and wanting so much to get the account that your palms sweat and you worry about saying the wrong thing each time you open your mouth. It is downright heartbreaking to make a mistake when you are close to a big account. However, in the beginning mistakes will happen, and you must accept their occurrence. If the same mistakes occur repeatedly, have your techniques analyzed by your superior.

One common mistake is to have a preconceived notion of what an investor should buy.

L.H. had been successful in making appointments with a series of dentists. He had entered each interview with the preconceived notion that they should invest in only blue chip securities. Many wished to speculate, and he got into arguments because he knew he was right and resented their refusal to agree with him. During one interview, a dentist said, "Being a dentist is rather boring (no pun intended). I like to speculate for excitement." L.H. now realized why the other dentists wished to speculate. Instead of arguing, he should have asked "Why?" In the future, he did so.

Firmness and Politeness Are the Rule

Since you must maintain control of the interview, the questions which the prospect asks you may throw you off track. After all, you do have a schedule of minimum and maximum objectives to obtain, and you cannot be swayed from your intent. The prospect will, perhaps as a subconscious defense mechanism, say things to lead you away from your objectives. He may start asking your opinions about various securities. Advise him that you do not wish to avoid the question, and that you will answer it later; that you have also made note of it for future reference, but for now the most important thing to find out is about his needs. He may start to tell you stories about friends who made or lost; about other brokers; about the stocks he could have bought at $5.00 which are $110.00 today. Advise him in each instance that his experiences are interesting but that both of you have the job of getting him invested properly. You might also tell him that Wall Street is full of stories, but that the only important story is himself—and doing the proper thing for him.

Be polite, and be firm. You will be unhappy as a broker if you let your customers run you. You must maintain control of them at all times, and the best place to start is in the beginning. Once the prospect senses that he can get the upper hand with you, he will have no respect for you and will not do business with you. Some individuals who maintain large accounts will attempt to treat you like a hired hand. People who are not used to wealth often use it to show their power. Where you meet such a person, recognize him for what he is, but preserve your personal prerogatives. If you are truly professional about your work, you need not take abuse from any customer. Sometimes you may overdo your tolerance of an account's abuse because of its size. *Be careful.*

K.R. had a substantial account. The husband was retired and the wife shared in his investment plans. They would berate K.R. at the slightest provocation. He was so afraid to lose this large account that he stood for their abuse. One day, K.R. had a nervous breakdown. He returned to work in two months, and on his doctor's advice he dropped the account. He is rebuilding a clientele. He's not as rich, but he's healthier and happier. He knows that riches will also come.

When you are satisfied that your interview is over, and when you, not the prospect, is satisfied, you can start on your presentation. If, during your analysis, you find you need more information, call the prospect and ask him for it. Don't be afraid to call people for any reason. Remember, your livelihood depends on the number of times you speak to people. And people don't resent being called if it is for their benefit.

The Seven Mistakes Most Often Made During Interviews

1. Letting the prospect grab control of the interview.
2. Failure to ask "Why?"
3. Failure to take notes during the interview.
4. Ending the interview inconclusively with no date set for a call back.

5. Becoming overly aggressive and antagonizing the prospect.
6. Making recommendations too hastily before having analyzed the prospect's requirements.
7. Failure to build a personal relationship.

CHAPTER 10

THE PRESENTATION

The Hidden Objection

Like everything else you do, the presentation must be prepared and organized. The more time you spend in organization, the less time you will spend in the prospect's office, and the sooner you will get the order. Prepare yourself for any eventuality and for any objection. Don't believe that your cogent analysis of the prospect's requirements and your astute choice of securities will make him open an account. The presentation must be designed to overcome the three hidden enemies of the representative: *fear, ignorance,* and *inertia.*

Your mind may be of the keenest, and your reasons for the prospect to open an account may be logically irrefutable, and yet he will refuse to do so. Unless you recognize the emotional factors, you will fail. Without turning this book into a treatise on psychology, suffice it to say that the people you meet will be moved by emotional factors as well as rational opinions. Too often the emotional factors obscure the rational opinions. Mr. Morris would like to invest, but why rush? There's always tomorrow. Mr. Finch remembers an uncle who lost money in 1929. And so, having gone through all the work of the interview and the analysis of his needs, you still have no assurance that the prospect will buy.

At this point, you yourself have some misgivings and wonder if you didn't make a mistake by coming into this business. Remember, your potential rewards are high and no one promised you that the reward would be yours for the asking. Remember also that we always said you would have to work for it.

The Four Steps to Opening the Account

The presentation can be divided into four parts. They are: Attention, Interest, Desire, and Action.

Initially, you must grasp the prospect's attention—fire his imagination and get his emotions working in favor of the product.

You cannot use flamboyant tactics to get attention. The securities business is still a sedate business, and yet, we are faced with the problem of people who should and could invest, but who are held back by fear and ignorance.

Let us assume that your prospect is a widow to whom dividends are important. You may get attention by saying: "Mrs. Brown, how would you like a summer vacation this year? You told me you have $10,000 to invest. Well, the securities I've selected would pay a current return of $460 a year. How does that appeal to you?"

If it is a businessman looking for "risk-type securities": "Mr. Morse, do you believe in taking sensible risks?" The answer would have to be "Yes." Or, "Mr. Morse, how would you like a sure thing guaranteed to go up 10 points?" Mr. Morse will say, "Of course." You then say, "I don't have any such thing, but I do know of a promising stock, the earnings of which are expected to increase 12 per cent; shall we talk about that?"

To the career girl who claims she could never accumulate money, you might say: "How would you like never to have to say, 'I don't have money'?" Proceed to tell her about a systematic investment plan.

To the man who is afraid to invest because he might lose his money, you might say: "Let's talk about your money in the bank. I can prove to you that you lost 25 per cent of the purchasing power of that money in the past 10 years. Would you like me to tell you how each $1000 in the bank is now worth $750 in purchasing power?"

Or, to the man who has two young children, "Would you like to see an investment plan which sent two children to college for the cost of one? It happened over the last ten years. Although we can't guarantee that the plan will do the same again, don't you think it's worth looking into?" (Send him information on the M.I.P. or Mutual Fund plan concurrent with the conversation.)

Your opening sentence must catch the imagination. It must attract attention and hold the prospect's interest in what else you have to say. The best way to get attention is to recognize from your analysis what it is that the prospect wants the most and focus your opening remarks on that point.

Don't Lie or Exaggerate

Although attention-getting remarks are exciting, they are honest and hold out no false promises. They are designed only to get the prospect's attention. It is impossible to enumerate the number of attention-getting remarks which may be made, because each remark must suit a specific instance. You, yourself, must be imaginative enough to invent attention-getting remarks. They may come to you at any time—make sure to write them down.

If you think of the opening remark as setting the mood for your presentation, you will be more successful. The opening scene of "Macbeth," with the three witches, tells us little, yet roots our attention. The opening sentence of your presentation may tell nothing, yet should attract the prospect to listen. Keep a list of good opening sentences and use them where appropriate.

Get the Prospect Involved in Your Story

And so, we have our prospect's attention. Our next goal is to *involve* him, to get his interest, to make him feel that what you are offering is for him. The interest will be based in the main on logical conclusions. There will be no attempt to offer anything except that which is logically correct for the prospect. If he needs income stocks, you point out the reasons why. If he needs growth stocks, you again point out the reasons why. It is during the "interest" portion that you may meet difficulty. Again, just as during the interview, you must maintain control of the presentation. The prospect will now ask you "Why?" He will also ask you extraneous questions designed to pull you away from your objectives. He will fight against you, not to avoid becoming a customer, but to make sure that you can provide enough arguments to prove your case.

The prospect who asks questions is a good prospect. The one who says nothing is a poor prospect. The prospect who makes you work does so because he is interested, but he wants to make sure that he's buying the right thing from the right person.

Prepare the Prospect to Be Positive

As you explain the merits of the securities selected for recommendation, obtain the prospect's agreement as you proceed with the presentation. For Mr. Benson, you selected a chemical company with long-term growth potential. You are now telling him of the company's past record: "Todd Chemical has increased its earnings by an average of 8% a year for the past five years. Isn't this the type company you should be interested in?" Wait for Mr. Benson's reply. It is important that you give him an opportunity to say "Yes." You then continue: "Todd Chemical has just added three new products to their sales line which should add to earnings and diversify their product line. This means more stability of income. Do you agree that this makes the company sounder?" Again, wait for a reply. Continue in this vein. As you enumerate the reasons why you made your choice, ask the prospect to comment on your opinion in a positive fashion.

Since every security has a negative side as well as a positive side, you will give the adverse opinions as well. In doing so, again get his reply, and then go into your "summation" where you will weigh the possible benefits against the possible risks.

The purpose of seeking positive answers is to involve the prospect in your story; to get his interest; and to make him think in a positive manner so that when you ask for the order, the word "yes" will come more readily.

Summarize Your Story

In your summation, you may very well say, "Mr. Benson, as the figures I've given you point out, the future for Todd Chemical is very promising. Don't you agree?"

Mr. Benson says, "Yes."

You continue: "There are, however, some possible adverse factors which have to be taken into consideration. Now, if the new product lines do not sell as well as anticipated, earnings may not reach new highs. Are you aware of this possibility, Mr. Benson?"

Mr. Benson replies "Yes."

"However, since the present price appears in line with present earnings, it would seem that a possible rise in price is worth the risk of the new products adding significantly to sales. Don't you, as a businessman, agree?"

Should Mr. Benson say yes, your next step is to ask for an order. He may, at this point, be reluctant to agree with you, or would wish more time to study your information.

Chances are you would not get an order at this point, but the attempt must be made and you must ask for the order. Every time an opportunity comes to ask for an order, do so. In all probability you will not get it until you've gone through the "desire and action" phase, but just as you must condition the prospect to say "Yes," you need to make him realize that you are seeking his business. Each time you ask for an order, you are letting him know that you are not seeking to waste his time or your time. Showing his firmness helped J.C., and the same attitude can help you.

J.C. had become registered at the age of 58. He knew many substantial businessmen. One in particular never gave him an order, although J.C. mailed him market letters and called him with information. Finally J.C. called him one day and said, "I'm calling for only one thing, and that is to find out why you have not done business with me?" The prospect had to admit there was no reason and opened an account.

Have These Props Ready

Since much of your presentation work is again being done via telephone, be sure to have a copy of the letter you sent to the prospect in front of you as you talk. Call his attention to sentences in the letter. It would be best to underline more important items prior to mailing the letter. By calling his attention to the sentences, you maintain control of the interview. If you see him in person, point out these items as you talk to hold his interest. Many research letters are too complicated for the average person to read. The Research Departments are to be commended on the splendid job they do, and competent work is taken for granted by the customer as well as the representative. Preface the complete report with a summary in a few sentences of the high spots which make each security worthy of recommendation. The prospect can then go on to read the complete story in the pages following your preface.

Having expressed our opinions as to the merits of our choice of securities, and having satisfactorily answered the prospect's questions, we still have to arouse his "desire" for the product, and get "action," or the order.

Caution

In whetting the customer's desire for the product, the registered representative must be careful not to breach the rules of ethical conduct. Desire is an emotional reaction, and in order to use it to overcome fear, ignorance, and inertia, we need to make desire the stronger emotion. To the man afraid to invest because he may lose money, you have to show him how he can lose money by *not* investing. For example, keeping excess money in a bank is like saying there will be no more inflation. If a man can be made to realize the risks of inflation, he can then weigh the risks of not investing vs. the risks of investing. Another method of overcoming fear is by appealing to another emotion—the emotional desire for wealth. This cannot be done, however, without bringing out the risks inherent in the search for wealth via the stock market.

Risk: the Price Paid for Profits

Your attitude towards *risk* must be positive. Risk is not something to be shunned. Risk must be accepted as a

necessary attribute to accomplishment. Nothing was ever
accomplished without risk. Whatever achievement a man
seeks must be accompanied by risk. Those who seek gain
must accept it, and those who accept safety and lack of
accomplishment shun it. Columbus took a risk to discover
America, and since that time the history of this country
has been written by those who sought risk and challenge
in order to make gains. The founding fathers: Adams, Jef-
ferson, Franklin, and Hamilton, were not penniless gam-
blers seeking to better themselves by way of revolution.
They were men of means who accepted risk as the price of
freedom. The pioneers who went west, and later, the im-
migrants from foreign countries, all accepted risk. Our
country and our economic system is the greatest in the
world because we have accepted risk for what it is—the
price to be paid for possible gains.

But risks, when taken, must be measured in proportion to the possible gain. One does not blindly gamble. One
weighs possibilities and probabilities before embarking on
a venture. Columbus had studied long before he made his
trip. He had some good ideas of where he was going, and
expected to find land. Ben Franklin was the most prudent
of men and he did not lightly set out on what appeared to
be a hopeless, idealistic course—the American Revolution
—which might have led to his being hanged. He, too, had
weighed the risks. Risk is in the American tradition.

Fair Play Is Also in the American Tradition

And so, too, must you measure out the possibilities.
It is not wrong to ask someone to take a risk. It is wrong,

however, not to advise him of the possibilities of losses as well as the possibilities of gains. You must play fair with your prospects and customers.

If, after competent research, you can argue that the possible appreciation in a security is worth the risk, then you can stimulate desire. Here, you, as the advisor to the prospect, must clearly interpret the research information and make it not only understandable to the prospect, but expressed so that he, too, can measure the risks against the rewards. In concrete terms, you could say, "This company has historically sold at 15 times its earnings. We expect earnings to rise by 50 cents a share in the coming year, and today's price, in our opinion, doesn't reflect that possible increase." If a company is working on a new product, you could, if possible, give the anticipated increase in earnings that it would bring. Bring the information down to basic and concrete terms. Needless to say, you are neither to make any promises nor make any statements not of a factual basis.

Breaking the Fear Barrier

By suggesting diversification, you help to alleviate fear. By investing in a selected few stocks rather than in one, you spread the risk. Diversification makes sense for the customer as well as for yourself. No one is smart enough to pick the one right security in each instance. By investing in several, you are probably sure to have some which will rise, as well as some which will not rise. On balance, you should be able to do a competent job by dropping out those which do not do well and replacing them.

You also overcome fear by reassuring the prospect

that you will maintain watch over his holdings. You must assure him that during the course of the day, you will keep his needs always in mind. This is only a part of your day-to-day job, and whereas you take it as a matter of course, he must be informed that you are prepared to watch his holdings for him. You might use this method to overcome fear:

K.H. had an account who was quite satisfied with his service. While on a call to a prospect's office, the prospect asked K.H. if he could talk to one of his accounts. K.H. thought of the satisfied account and suggested the man call, although he had no idea how his account would react. The account was pleased to do him the favor, and did so many other times.

Ask one of your accounts if he will permit prospects to call him to inquire about your services. Get the prospect to call this customer for an opinion about yourself.

You Are Also an Educator

When you come upon the person who has money but is ignorant about investing, you take on the job of educator. Usually, as the prospect learns about investing, he gets the desire to invest—provided that you can satisfactorily answer all his questions. The education process can include information given by yourself in conversation as well as printed matter on investing. Several pamphlets provided by the New York Stock Exchange are excellent for this purpose. *Understanding the New York Stock Exchange* and *Does It Make Sense for Me to Buy Stocks,* are two such pamphlets for which you will have a great deal of use.

CHAPTER **11**

LIFTING THE IRON CURTAIN OF INERTIA

HAVING CREATED A DESIRE FOR THE PRODUCT, we are now prepared to ask for the order. But the prospect is still reluctant to buy and we have to stimulate him to action. We have overcome fear and ignorance, and now we have to overcome inertia—the human capability for standing pat and doing nothing, on the assumption that if you don't make a move, you can't make a mistake.

When you say, "Mr. Benson, you agree this is the security for you. Give me your order for 100 shares," Benson can reply with any one of these standard objections:

1. I haven't read the literature yet.
2. I must talk it over with my (choose one): wife, accountant, lawyer, brother, partner, uncle.

3. The market is too high.

4. I don't want to take my money out of the bank. I'll lose interest now. Wait until the end of the quarter.

5. Stocks are going down.

6. I have a broker.

7. I'll call you back on it.

8. I'll wait and see if it goes up.

9. I don't have any money.

10. I want to wait until after (choose one): the strike is over, the election is over, Christmas, Easter, the crisis, the war scare, etc.

Your replies to each objection could be:

1. Mr. Benson, if you have to read the information over again, I've done a poor job of explaining. What precisely don't you understand?

2. Talking it over with your accountant is fine, let me give him the facts about Todd Chemical. What is his name and number?

3. We're not talking about buying the whole market. Granted it is higher than it has ever been, but Todd Chemical is behind the market, in our opinion, and could catch up, because. . . .

4. We think Todd Chemical is a good buy at today's price. By the end of the month the opportunity may not exist any more. It may be worthwhile to forego the few dollars in interest; I think you should act now.

5. At all times some stocks are going down, while others are going up. We're not going to discuss a purchase of all stocks. We are talking about one company which

we have studied very carefully and which we consider an excellent profit opportunity at this time.

6. I'm sure he's a good man, too, but two heads are better than one. The information I give you may not be available to him. When I have a recommendation of special interest, may I call you to tell you about it?

7. Mr. Benson, how many times have you said to someone, "I'll call you back," and then forgotten to do so. Todd Chemical looks attractive now. I suggest you do not wait too long.

8. Mr. Benson, I think it makes good sense to check and see if my information works out, but my firm has serviced thousands of investors and we would not be in business today if we hadn't done a satisfactory job. We recommend Todd Chemical, and I think you should own some. We've already gone over the records. How many shares do you want?

9. How would you like to never have to say the words "I don't have money," ever again. Though there is never a guarantee of investment return, I can suggest a way to accumulate money. (Arrange to see him for an M.I.P. or Mutual Funds plan.)

10. The past 10 years have been a period of rising prices, and during these years we had Christmases, a war in Hungary, a Cuban crisis, and three elections. You are just afraid to invest. What do you fear? (Bring out the true reason why he isn't investing so that you may answer it.)

Get Behind the Smoke Screen

Very often the objection voiced by the prospect is not the true objection. He will throw up a smoke screen to hide his real motive for not buying. You will have to learn which objections are valid and which are devised to get rid of you. You can tell it is a false objection if it does not fit into the framework of what you know about the person. Very often, it is just your neglecting the wife that holds up the order.

T.M. had called on a prospect several times, and had presented a suggested portfolio which suited the prospect's needs—the prospect even admitted to this fact. But each time T.M. asked for the order he was given various excuses from the above list. However, T.M. felt he knew the prospect well enough to realize that the excuses were not valid. After several calls back, the prospect finally admitted that T.M. was right, but he was afraid to invest without his wife's approval, and he had been ashamed to admit this fact! T.M. suggested they speak to the wife together. She agreed to invest, but for a lesser amount than anticipated.

The Two Main Objections

The objections raised the most to keep you from calling back are: (1) "I have a broker," and (2) "I don't have any money." You will meet these objections only if your tactics have been too high-pressured, and if you have failed to give satisfactory reasons for your recommendations. If you find yourself getting the above two objections, you had better review your sales tactics.

Ask for the Sale Indirectly

When the time comes to actually ask for the order, you can do so indirectly or directly. An indirect approach would be to say, "Shall we buy 100 shares in your name or in joint account with your wife?" Another indirect approach is, "Shall we buy in a cash or in a margin account?" The indirect approach assumes consent and gives a choice as to *how* the purchase shall be made, and not *whether* it shall be made. The direct approach is simply saying, "Will you buy 100 shares?"

You might very well at this juncture get an order. If the answer is "No," it means you didn't do a good job somewhere along the line. Just like an electrician faced with a blown fuse, you have to track down where the trouble is located. Was it in your approach, your presentation, or in your closing? Sometimes the prospect will identify the problem. Ask him directly why he doesn't like your choice. Bring all the objections out in the open where you can answer them.

In closing the sale, you must be careful not to make yourself obnoxious by being too overbearing. You will be able to sense resistance to your method building up in the client if you are using pressure. Back down and disengage yourself from the conversation, but leave the way open for a call back at an early date.

Friendly Persuasion, Not Argumentation

Under *no* circumstances are you to argue with the prospect. Many people use argument as a defense method. This is done subconsciously. It is their way of refusing to act. Do not get dragged into a vehement discussion. The best way to handle the argumentative person is to let him blow off steam and then continue with your presentation.

Where the individual is unreasonable, point out his unreasonableness.

After the demand for action has been made, and you are unable to open the account, you must have failed either to arouse interest or create desire; in other words, you either failed to point out his investment needs or you failed to prove to him that these were his true needs. You will have to review your conversation and ascertain just where you made your error. Arrange for a call back, and use the intervening time to determine what you did that was wrong.

Look for Clues to Your Lost Sales

H.G. had spent considerable time preparing a portfolio for a prospect. He had also prepared his presentation very carefully, and seemed to have the prospect's agreement all during the interview. At the close, the prospect refused to buy, and H.G. could not get any reason except "I want to wait a few weeks. My affairs are unsettled now." H.G. was puzzled by the difference between the warm reception he had received at the beginning of the interview and the coldness evident at the close. He discussed his prospect with his manager, who was able to point out the error made by H.G. In an early conversation, the prospect had told H.G. he was dissatisfied with his present broker because he had suggested sales of certain securities after they had had a brief rise. During the interview, the prospect had asked H.G. what should be done if the recommendations rose. H.G., without thinking of the import of the question, had answered, "It might be wise to sell." From that point on in the interview, H.G. could no longer get his message through to the prospect. He was unable to call back on this man and had to consider it a lesson well-learned.

Those Loaded Questions!

When you are asked questions, do not take them at their face value. What may appear to be innocuous to you may be of extreme significance to the prospect. Hesitate before replying to each question, and try to determine the real reason why it is being asked. Your prospect will cross-examine you to determine whether you are the right man for him. If the significance of a question escapes you, then ask the prospect why he asked this question. The prospect may say, "Do you work with charts?" Although this sounds like a reasonable and intelligent question, let us try to determine why it was asked. Here are some possible reasons: (1) the prospect believes in their use and would like to use them; (2) the prospect believes they are of some use but insists on fundamental knowledge as well; or (3) the prospect has had a poor experience with charts and would rather not use them. Since you do not know which reason prompted this question, before answering, find out what he thinks about charts. If he remains noncommittal, as a means of further testing you, then you must reply and adhere to the truth. If you are an out and out chartist, you will have to tell him so and take your chances on convincing him that you are a capable interpreter of chart formations. If you use both technical and fundamental factors, advise him so. If you are strictly a fundamentalist and he prefers charts, you could agree to check outside recommendations from charts for his personal convenience. Because your ideas don't coincide with the customer's ideas, it doesn't mean that you should change your way of thinking to suit him. If you find yourself trying to think the way 100 different people think, you will lose all control of your accounts. Their thinking must coincide with yours. You are to be the guiding influence. In replying to a prospect's questions about your investment beliefs and attitudes, don't bend your beliefs to get the account.

Sincerity Shows

O.M. had an excellent faculty for simulating interest in the customer's investment wants. He adhered to *wants* only and never probed to find the investor's *needs*. By catering to wants he attracted customers readily, but just as soon lost them. One customer, the wife of a wealthy physician, was a good example of the problem. She insisted on short-term trading, and invariably lost money. O.M. did not try to talk to her about long-range investing. She had already used six brokers previously, none of whom tried to reason with her. (Whether or not she *could* be reasoned with is another matter.) He got the account, but lost it after the first trade at a loss. Don't act unless you are prepared to act sincerely.

CHAPTER 12

HOW GOOD IS THE ORDER?

LET US ASSUME THAT YOU HAVE LEARNED YOUR lessons well and have been able to open the account. You are now faced with another problem, "How good is the order?"

There are certain individuals who literally sit up nights trying to figure out ways to cheat brokerage firms. There are others who do so periodically, or when prompted by a sudden drop in their purchases. Should a man who just bought 100 shares of a $50 stock see a drop of five points before settlement date, the idea may burst into his head that he could deny having given the order, would not pay, and could save himself $500! Although a very small percentage of customers may do so, consider the risk that you and your firm take with each order—for a commission of $44 there is the risk of losing several hundred dollars, unless you really "know your customer."

The customer who is apt to back out on payment is either a "bad actor," who knowingly bought with the intention of not paying if the stock went down, or, most likely, a customer who was pressured into buying. One of the great dangers of "high-pressure selling" is that the customer may very well not pay. He will feel as though he has been "taken" and will not pay on the settlement date.

It then becomes a matter of your word against his, and if he denies having placed the order, you are not only faced with financial loss, but possible charges of having placed a fictitious order!

The problem of "how good is the order" does not only revolve around your new accounts, but also concerns established accounts. Whenever an account has not been serviced properly, that account is a potential non-payer! If you recommend a stock to an established account which is of a type not suitable for his requirements, you run the risk of non-payment, as well as the loss of the entire account.

Where a new account wishes to place a large order, caution is certainly called for, and where an established account places an order above his customary amounts of purchase, caution is again called for. The customer who bought 20-share lots and now places orders for 200-share lots should be diplomatically questioned as to the source of his new-found money.

Be cautious about new friends or individuals who come to your office and who make a point of appearing affluent. They may tell about sizeable holdings, great profits made, expensive resorts visited, rich friends, and regale you with all the outward signs of wealth. This person may very well be setting you up for a large order which will not be paid for if the stock goes down. Every new account, no matter how wealthy he seems, should only be allowed a reasonable amount of credit, and unhesitatingly be asked to make a deposit with the purchase. When you pick up a check, don't accept it if it is drawn on an out-of-town bank. There is no reason for a resident of your city to maintain an account in a bank in another city—do not accept any reason, no matter how plausible, for this phenomenon.

It is good business practice to ask a new account for an immediate deposit under all circumstances. Where the issues are of a volatile nature, it is incumbent upon yourself to get a substantial down-payment, either before placing the order, or certainly soon after. If you receive an order to buy a volatile issue, show it to your manager or partner at once and ask what to do. Each firm has its own rules, but most firms will require an immediate deposit. This means that you may have to leave the office at once to pick up a check from the customer. This effort is well worth the trouble. The sharp operator usually looks for the inexperienced representative—one who is so eager to get an order that he will tend to overlook the risk to the firm. Although most firms have safeguards against accepting large orders without a deposit or a thorough credit check, do not accept large orders without advising the customer that the order is subject to your receipt of money immediately. The honest customer does not resent what is only good business practice. Only the man who is trying to get away with something will put up a fuss.

The Small, Subtle Thieves

Besides giving you orders which will not be honored, an account can deprive you of money in more subtle ways. During your interview, watch out for the account which will require more time than necessary for the business which is to be derived from him. A small account who demands a great deal of attention is not worth your time; an account who will be easily upset and seek to berate you if your recommendations don't work out, is also not worth your time. You will have to appropriate time to placating him which should be spent in more productive efforts. Make sure your account understands and accepts risks. Look for those signs which show an argumentative and unreasonable attitude. If your prospect is difficult to reason with, don't accept him as a customer. The pressure of the securities business is great enough without assuming troublesome accounts.

CHAPTER **13**

THE PRODUCTS YOU HAVE TO OFFER

THE MORE YOU DIVERSIFY THE TYPES OF IN-
vestments you sell, the larger and more stable
will your earnings be. The registered representative who solicits stock business only, finds
his income curtailed during dull markets. The
Registered Representative who seeks out bond
customers, mutual fund customers, put and
call customers, as well as stock customers is
broadening the sources of his income. The ever-
present stock ticker makes us focus our attention on stocks. But we do not work in a business with just one product to offer. We have
many products for many types of investors.
One registered representative found an excellent source of commissions in a very uncom-
mon security, Savings & Loan accounts.

T.M. had noticed certain investment firms
offering to place money for interested parties

[143]

into Savings & Loan accounts. T.M. investigated and found out that Savings & Loan companies paid commissions for such placements. He spoke to his firm and they allowed him to solicit such accounts through them. Although this is hardly the type of investment one associates with a member firm, T.M. was able to build a substantial business in all types of securities from initially offering Savings & Loan accounts.

Sell the Complete Line

The routine of doing business in stocks to the exclusion of other security types is easy to fall into, and one must fight against it. Make the effort to learn about bonds, options, mutual funds, and commodities. Each facet of the business which you learn broadens your income base.

For the long-term investor, your offer can be "blue chip stocks" and Mutual Funds.

For the trader, you can offer volatile stocks, special situations, cyclical issues, options, and commodities.

For the investor seeking income, you can offer bonds, quality dividend-paying stocks, and Mutual Funds.

For the investor wishing to make periodic payments, there are the M.I.P. and systematic investment plans in Mutual Funds, with or without decreasing term life insurance.

Regular Income for Yourself

One of the best ways to provide steady income is to sell, wherever possible, some form of systematic investment plan. As the investors make their payments each month, you are provided with a steady source of income. Each commission is small but as your accounts grow, in the aggregate, the money coming in each month gets larger and larger. If you intend to stay in this business a long time, you should start soliciting periodic investment accounts immediately in order to assure a steady source of income month after month. This type of investor is not concerned with the vagaries of the market and will make payments through all kinds of investment weather.

As an example of how systematic investment commissions can act as a cushion to your income, let us assume that you sell one Mutual Fund investment plan every two weeks, which calls for a $100 a month investment. Your net, under present schedules, will approximate:

At the end of one year	$ 72	each month
At the end of two years	144	each month
At the end of three years	216	each month
At the end of four years	288	each month

These plans will not make you rich, but you cannot think only in terms of the big commission. Your paycheck is an accumulation of items large and small, derived from all the categories of investment available. You never know when the small sale may lead to the large sale, as it did for W.N., a female registered representative who had opened a small account for her neighbor. He couldn't invest much money because he needed the money for his business. His business grew and reached the point to where an underwriting was called for. He asked W.N. to handle it. She brought the proposition to her firm and they liked it. They came out with a new issue on which she received a substantial commission.

Don't Neglect Your High Tax Bracket Customer!

Although municipal bonds are a volume item and are usually moved in large numbers through institutional accounts, there are many individuals who buy municipal bonds because of the tax-saving feature. In analyzing your accounts and prospects, do not overlook the possibilities for municipal bonds. To any of your accounts in higher tax brackets, they are meaningful.

Options are for the speculator as well as for the investor seeking to hedge his position. They are an old investment tool, dating back some 400 years. If you need knowledge of options, any one of the option dealers will provide you with complete information and assist you in developing your option business.

To deal in options, however, requires a degree of knowledge beyond that which the average registered representative usually receives. You will have to make an intensive study; for this purpose, many of the option dealers have study material and even study courses. Ideally, you should work options into your regular stock business.

Share in the Mutual Fund Boom

Mutual Funds have proven to have wide customer acceptance. Sales continue at consistently high volume, and no registered representative should ignore their appeal. They are an excellent item to be sold after market hours. For late afternoon and evening sales they are ideal. Their attraction is to the new and unsophisticated investor, although the larger sales are usually made to those who already are stockholders. In a survey among Mutual Fund shareholders made a few years ago, the most important reason they gave for investing in Mutual Fund shares was the diversification afforded.

Since there are a great many funds, the representative usually is at a loss as to where to start. If your firm has a fund specialist, he will, of course, help you. If not, look over the past records of several funds, and those which appeal to you can be made the basis for your sales approach. The fund will have a wholesale representative in your area and he will be willing to help you with literature, sales ideas, and even personal assistance on your calls. You do not obligate yourself; he's pleased to have the opportunity to help.

There are many ways to sell Mutual Funds, including outright cash investments, level payment plans, contractual plans, systematic withdrawal plans, and letters of intention.

A Sample Mutual Fund Sales Approach

Where an investment in Mutual Funds is indicated, the sales technique can receive assistance from the sales literature issued by the Mutual Fund-sponsoring companies. Each Fund has a brochure giving its past record of performance, and is, of course, to be used only with prior or concurrent delivery of the prospectus. The sales message will have to follow the pattern of *attention, interest, desire,* and *action.* The following is a sales method for each part of the sales pattern given above:

ATTENTION (Show the Past Record)

Mr. Prospect, here is the past record of Alpha Mutual Fund. An investment of $10,000 made 10 years ago, with all distributions reinvested, would be worth $35,000 today. Of course that record is for the past 10 years only, in a period of rising prices, and future results may be more or less, but doesn't a record like that merit your consideration? (Wait for a reply.)

INTEREST

Mr. Prospect, wouldn't you like to know just how Alpha Fund grew in value? (Wait for a reply. Open sales brochure to list of Alpha Fund's holdings and point to them.)

Alpha Fund invested its shareholders' money in such fine companies as (read from list) Ford, I.B.M., R.C.A., Dupont, and other leading firms. Would you lose sleep nights if your money were invested in such companies? (Wait for answer.) Over the past 10 years these investments grew in value and also paid dividends. Of course, I cannot guarantee that they will do so in the next 10 years. However, the dividends were reinvested and allowed to grow with the original investment. Now, Alpha Fund works on the principle not only of diversification—that is, spreading investment risk over a great many companies (run your hand over the list of companies to illustrate)—but Alpha also has professional management to supervise the holdings and to make changes when they think necessary. No one stock is the perfect investment, and if management thinks Ford should be replaced by General Motors, or Dupont by Dow Chemical, those changes are made for you—you have no investment problems to solve—the professionals of Alpha management do it for you, and their fee is only .5 percent of the annual assets. Wouldn't you like to have your own personal investment portfolio managed by professionals? (Wait for an answer.)

DESIRE

Mr. Prospect, most people have some goal they dream of

attaining: enough money to retire comfortably; enough money to send children to college; enough money to start their own business. (Write these three items on a pad in front of the prospect.) Which one of these is your ambition? (Wait for an answer.) Mr. Prospect, Alpha Fund may be of help to you in reaching your goal. No investment is guaranteed as to future success, but if you believe that sound investments will continue to grow in value, and if you have enough confidence in the American economy and the ability of Alpha's management to select securities in that economy carefully, then you should invest! How much were you considering investing? (Wait for an answer.)

ACTION

Mr. Prospect, shall I open the account in joint name with your wife? Or as a Custodian for your child?

Of course, it is much easier to write a presentation than it is to make one in person, but the salesman must maintain control over the interview. There will be objections and efforts made to stall the salesman. But recognize these for what they are—a healthy desire to make you prove your points. Some of the more likely objections are:

OBJECTIONS	ANSWERS
Is it guaranteed?	No investment is guaranteed. Why even your dividends at the bank are not guaranteed. However, unlike the bank, Mutual Fund shares fluctuate up or down.
Can I get my money out?	Yes, you can redeem your shares at the market value which will be more or less than your investment at any time.

The sales charge is too high.	If you invested that same amount of money in several stocks, it would cost you as much or more, especially as you bought and sold to make changes.
I think I'll wait.	Wait for what? Anyone who waited during the past 20 years lost his opportunity. I don't want you to lose what may be yours—how much do you wish to invest now?
The market is going down! *or,* The market is too high!	No one really knows if the market is high or low, but to make sure you catch the market in any event, let's invest half now and half in a few months. How much is half of your intended investment?

When a periodic investment is indicated, you can suggest the level payment plan or the contractual plan. The level payment plan has no front end load. However, it requires an investor who will make payments in accordance with his original intentions. Those who do not need a forced method of accumulating money, should use the level payment plan. Those who need discipline should consider using the contractual plan.

The Plan Presentation

You may start by saying (using a Fund's past record), "Mr. Prospect, this is the past record of a 10-year systematic investment program in Alpha Fund. Of course, this was a period of rising prices, and future results may be more or less, but doesn't a record like this merit your consideration?" (Wait for answer.) "Mr. Prospect, there was a cost for this investment, and that cost was $960, most of which was taken out month by month in the program's first year. It amounted to half the first year's payments. This means that if an investor stopped this plan in the early years he would surely take a loss. Now, I'd like to ask you a question. If you undertook such an investment program, do you believe you would have to stop it in the early years?" If the answer is "yes," then tell the investor the plan is not for him.

The *interest, desire,* and *action* sections are the same as previously given. The objections will also be similar.

You Will Be Asked Questions

The most frequently asked questions are:

Q. Can I get money out at any time?
A. Yes, at the market value. However, this plan has a partial liquidation feature which means that you can take out part of your money and replace it at a later date.

Q. What happens if I stop my payments?
A. You don't lose the plan. The money you put in, less charges, will be working for you. You can continue your payments at any time. Remember, this is not a 10-year plan—it's a 120-payment plan. You can make a payment a week, a payment a month, or every two months. You can even skip a whole year without a payment. But that will never help you reach your goal.

Q. How do I pay taxes on the dividends?
A. At the end of the year, the fund sends you a statement of the amount of dividends and profits you received. Place the information in your tax form and that will do it.

Q. What will my plan be worth in the next 10 years?

A. No one can tell. However, the past records have been favorable. Here are the past results. (Show records for past periods in the Fund's history.)

Because many Mutual Funds are a long-term investment, and many are suitable for such long-term objectives as retirement and education plans, representatives sometimes neglect to see their use for the inactive investor seeking income.

Income—the Great Attraction

Among your accounts will be many who primarily seek income. They will not trade and will often be neglected for your more active accounts. Of course, they'll be in quality stocks, but every account requires supervision. Instead of taking your time to supervise these accounts, it would be better to suggest a Mutual Fund with the objective of paying income. There are many such Funds doing an excellent job in this respect, and in placing the investor in an income type Fund, you will be releasing your time for more productive work. Usually, besides the income dividends, there is an added capital gains distribution which is welcomed by the investor. Select an income Fund and work with the Fund's distributor. He'll assist you with literature and ideas.

The systematic withdrawal plan can now be presented. Figures are now available for past performance. Sales of such plans are large and tap a market of which the average representative usually never dreams. Essentially, the investor invests a sum of not less than $10,000 and will receive a fixed sum each month to be derived from dividends, profits, and capital. The investor is faced, therefore, if the withdrawal is too large, with eventual erosion of principal. Strangely enough, a great many elderly people are not overly worried about this prospect—they are more concerned with leaving anything over; they want to live for all they're worth.

And so, presenting systematic withdrawal plans, even with the apparent drawback of possible loss of capital, does not faze the investor. Those who choose the withdrawal plan prefer the fixed sum each month, which the plan provided, to varying dividends from an investment which does not eat into the principal. Since the usual minimum sale is $10,000, such sales, even if not made frequently, can provide a good source of income to the representative. Needless to say, the investor should be cautioned about drawing too large an amount each month.

Profit-Sharing Plans: A Door-Opener

Again, the Funds have done the job of preparing the material necessary for Profit-Sharing Plans. Such plans can invest in stocks also, and need not be confined to Mutual Funds—but the modus operandi will be found among the Mutual Fund promotional literature. The attraction of the Profit-Sharing Plan is that it helps keep employees with the corporation and also provides the officers with a retirement plan with a built-in tax-saving feature. The payment to the plan, which is made only in a profitable year, is deductible to the corporation, and the earnings of the Profit-Sharing Plan are not taxed, but are left to compound. (You may never sell one Profit-Sharing Plan, but they do make excellent means of getting to speak to corporate officers who may become customers for common stocks.) You may also very well start several Profit-Sharing Plans which will become a source of continuous income over the years.

The Big, Big Sale

If you stay on the alert for possible candidates for underwritings, you may come up with a handsome commission. In your prospecting be on the look-out for promising young companies who could benefit from going public. Bring them to the attention of your firm, and you may make one year's salary right there! You may only close one such deal in five years—but always remember to look for them. Be sure the company has a desirable product, competent management, and every attribute needed for success except adequate invested capital.

By diversifying your product line, you will be insuring yourself of larger and more continuous commissions, even if every commission is not large.

We all like to see home runs when we go to the ball game. But the singles, doubles, and even the bases on balls can do more to win a ball game than the more spectacular home run. Learn to make *every* kind of hit. Each one counts.

CHAPTER 14

THE COLD CALL

MOST CANDIDATES FOR THE STOCK BROKERAGE business do not anticipate making cold calls. It is an activity more readily associated with the encyclopedia salesman or vacuum cleaner salesman. Let us not, however, disparage these other salesmen. They have done a phenomenal job of selling their products, and not because they made cold calls, but because they were aware of the fundamental principle of all selling— *you only get results when you talk to people.* Tell your story to as many persons as possible and you will get sales. Why should we, who have a much finer product to sell, not take our story to the American people? The image of the stockbroker is that of a man somewhat aloof from the general public. This picture may have been correct some 30 years ago, but it is not correct today. Public participation in the stock

[155]

market is at an all-time high. Today's American has surplus money which his father and grandfather never dreamed of having. Today's American works a shorter workweek and has surplus funds above his daily needs. But, because he most usually comes from a family background where investing was unheard of, he never met a broker. The man who is 40 years old today and earning a decent income was raised during the depression years. Chances are his family did not even have a bank account, and he has no tradition of investing in his family background. If anything, he is ignorant of investments. His money is in a savings account where it earns interest. He comprehends interest. He understands that he can be paid for the use of his money. He realizes that the borrowee of money earns interest. He does not realize the possible benefits of owning securities; that as an owner of a company he may share in its good, as well as bad, fortune. He is ignorant of the facts of investing and will not willingly go to see a broker, either because he believes a broker is out of his class, or because he feels the few thousand dollars he has available for investment are not worth bothering about.

There is also the man who has invested, but whose broker is not doing a competent job. He is not getting the service he merits. How are you to go about meeting these people in order to tell them what you can do for them? Of course, you can make innumerable calls on the telephone, or send out innumerable mailing pieces, but there is one short, forthright method of meeting people, and that is to call on them *directly!*

There Is No Competition in Making Cold Calls

At this juncture you may say, "What kind of nonsense is this? I'm a stockbroker. How will I look calling on strangers? Certainly not!" *There* is the first reason why you should make cold calls. Most brokers feel the same way, and, therefore, very few do it. The path is wide open for the man who makes the effort. Not only do few brokers make cold calls, but those who do achieve excellent results. The people they call on are taken completely by surprise; in most instances are delighted to learn that brokers are human, and go calling on people like any other salesman.

For the new representative, cold calling should be a *must*. He will come across many different situations, and learn how to master them. He will sharpen his selling techniques and become an effective salesman so much sooner. But prior to making cold calls, one should prepare oneself.

Cold calling requires considerable physical stamina. Be prepared to undertake a difficult physical job and pace yourself accordingly. Start in with a few hours work each day, and then, if you are up to it, a whole day. Select your area of operations. Try to stay as close to your office as possible. You may find business in your own building as I did.

The writer started with a firm located on the corner of Broadway and Wall Street. One day his manager, seeing him sitting around the office, suggested he make some calls in the building—a building 50 percent populated by brokers! He complied, and called on several offices. There was a lawyer's office directly above. The lawyer had never spoken to a broker before, was glad for the opportunity, and later opened an account!

Be Versatile in Your Approach

Having selected the area where you wish to canvass, prepare your introductory remarks. Do not start out with any preconceived notions of what you will say, but get ready for any eventuality. You will meet an infinite variety of people and investment needs. Get ready to answer any and all questions. Your opening words should not be overly dramatic, nor should they be too strong. Even though you are making cold calls, you are still the "staid stockbroker." Of course, your dress and bearing is in keeping with the general opinion of what the broker should look like. You are dressed neatly and conservatively. Your hair is cut and your shoes are shined. You do not enter any office smoking a cigarette or with your hat on.

The purpose of the cold call is to get qualified prospects, which means that after you leave a man's office you will know whether or not he is a prospect, and if he is a prospect that he is a reasonably good one. You will not spend your time in idle chitchat, but in discussing the matter which brought you to his office—his investment needs, if any.

Your personal attitude will be a deciding factor in your success. Do not make cold calls with the attitude that you are doing something beneath your dignity. You won't get very far. Approach the cold call as though you were a missionary bringing a message of enlightenment to those less fortunate than you—those who are uninformed about the risks and rewards of common stock investment. Your message can make a great change in that man's life. He can be shown how to share in the earnings of American industry. He may be one of the many Americans who look upon speculation as a necessary adjunct to the possible attainment of wealth, and who is willing to take the chance of losses in order to make profits. He may have no one to guide him, or he may have someone with whom he is dissatisfied. You may meet a conservative person who is seeking income, or a young person to whom long-term capital growth has meaning. No matter whom you meet, you will be able to assist them with their financial problem. You are not going to meet people just to earn a commission. You are going to meet people whom you can aid. If you can't help them, you won't do business with them. If you can help them, you'll show them how and why so that they will understand the reasons.

Take with you as few papers as possible, preferably just some note paper and a few market letters placed in your pocket. Don't carry a brief case. Most secretaries are trained to turn away the man with the brief case because it is the unmistakable sign of the salesman.

Finding Your Man Is Easy

As to the man you wish to see, you will find his name either on the board in the lobby of the building, or on the door of the office you will enter. When you come into the office, you will inevitably be met by a receptionist. Don't pull any "gimmicks." As quietly and politely as possible, tell her your name as you hand her a card and that you are from a member firm of the New York Stock Exchange or the N.A.S.D., giving her the name of the firm. Since most receptionists presume that their bosses are well-off, she probably will call the boss and ask if he will see you. She will rarely send you away without first checking with her superior. If the boss wants to know why you came to call, you may offer any one of the following reasons:

> 1. I'm from the investment broker firm of _____, just down the block, and we are calling on businessmen in the area to offer an appraisal of their holdings. There's no charge. What stocks do you have that we can check into for you?
> 2. Our firm, a member of the New York Stock Exchange, puts out a popular Market Letter. I'm here to show you a copy and to ask if you'd like to receive the next four issues at no cost. Would you care to receive it? (Wait for an answer and, whether it is "yes" or "no," ask if he'd like to receive your evaluation of the securities he now holds.)
> 3. I have with me our list of current recommendations. You may care to go over it and compare your holdings with our present suggestions. Can I take 10 minutes of your time to show it to you?

You can make up your own "door opener" sentences. They must be courteous, and make a reasonable offer to which the prospect can respond without feeling under pressure to act. Sometimes ingenuity can help you get an interview. Here's how quick thinking helped one man:

F.V. had made a practice of cold calling in the vicinity of his office, and had become expert at it. On one call, he found himself in the anteroom of a glass-enclosed office.

He gave his card to the secretary who walked into the glass-enclosed office, and F.V. saw her hand it to her boss. He then saw the boss tear up his card and send the secretary out to him. She told him the boss wouldn't see him. F.V. rose to the challenge. If the boss wouldn't see him, he shouldn't, however, have torn up his card! F.V. asked the secretary to return his card inasmuch as it cost money, and asked the secretary to go and get it. The secretary went to the boss and F.V. saw her talk to him. He then saw him take out a coin from his pocket and give it to her. The secretary came out and handed F.V. a nickel, saying it was for his card. F.V. then gave the secretary another card, saying "this is for your boss, they're two for a nickel!" The secretary brought the second card into her boss. F.V.'s ingenuity was too much for him; he asked the secretary to bring him in.

Don't Overlook the Secretary

If you can't get to see the boss, or even if you do see him, don't overlook the secretary. Have with you some information on M.I.P. or a Mutual Fund plan that you can leave with her. Many married women work, and together with their husbands earn a substantial income. They may know little about investing, but if they are informed, may become accounts, especially for some form of systematic investment. Sometimes the secretary has money and the boss does not, as R.J. found out. R.J. had called by appointment on an executive of a linen company. The executive turned out to be one of those people who live beyond their means and had no money for investment. He had hoped by this meeting to learn how to save money. R.J. discussed a systematic investment plan, which although not a savings plan, would call upon him to put some money away each month. The executive just couldn't set aside a penny for it. As R.J. left the office, the secretary, who had been close enough to hear everything, followed him out and said that she had been looking for this herself. She came to R.J.'s office the next day to open an account.

Be Brief on Your Initial Cold Call

When you are called in to see the man you came to call on, assure him that your stay will be brief. Show him the material you have to offer and ask him to read it at his leisure and that you'll maintain him on your mailing list for a certain period. Don't offer your material on an indefinite basis—it makes it seem too easy to get and, therefore, undesirable. Take out a small pad of white paper and say, "Perhaps I can be of help to you in other ways. What securities do you hold now?" Wait for an answer. Continue to ask more questions, such as "What price did you pay for each security? Have you bought haphazardly or with some over-all purpose in mind? What would you say your investment objectives are?" You may have to answer several questions yourself before you will get the answers you seek from the prospect. He will want to make sure that he is talking to someone competent, and he may ask you about your background. He may also ask your opinion about certain stocks as a means of testing you. Although there are over 1200 stocks listed on the New York Stock Exchange, most people, without realizing the enormity of the job, expect you to have some knowledge of the stock they ask you about. When you are asked about a stock, and if you know the answer, tell it. But if you do not know the answer, explain the impossibility of keeping tabs on 1200 stocks, but through the research facilities available to you, you'll call back next morning with an answer. Even more dramatically, ask for permission to use his phone, call your Research Department right from his desk, and supply him with the answer. The prospect is not too concerned with your knowing the answer at once. He is more concerned with your ability to get the information as quickly as possible.

Get Personal to Build a Firmer Relationship

Do not confine your questions to investment subjects. Ask him where he lives, and if you know someone in his area, inquire if he knows them. Also ask about his family and his business. In short, treat him as you would any prospect, but do not try to make a sale on this, your first visit. No man will open an account with a complete stranger who just walked in the door. He will want to know him better. And, no registered representative wants to open an account for a complete stranger whom *he* has just met, without also knowing something about the man.

Don't stay in the prospect's office more than 20 minutes. This is sufficient time for both of you to get acquainted. If you try to stay longer, you will be wearing out your welcome, and if he tries to keep you longer, make sure of his motives. He may only try to keep you so long as you supply him with free information. You must be careful about dispensing your knowledge. You spend a great deal of time studying. Do not give that information away easily which you work so hard to obtain. The prospect will have little respect for you if you tell him all you know without making any demands on him in return.

You Now Have a Prospect

When you leave the cold call prospect's office, you will have gathered some information about him. There may be just enough information to keep within your minimum goal of maintaining him on a mailing list, to your maximum goal of attaining enough information to do an analysis and come back with a presentation. In either event, get his permission. Make sure he expects to get further mail from you, or that he expects you to call back with suggestions for his portfolio. If you are coming back, make a definite appointment. When you get back to your office, make out a Prospect Card in his name and place the appointment in your diary.

When you leave the office, thank his secretary or receptionist. She'll remember you, and when you call again, will make it easy for you to see or talk to the prospect.

How to Overcome "Post-Cold Call Coolness"

Very often on your call back you will find your greeting not as cordial as when you saw the man the first time. This "post-cold call coolness" is caused by the prospect's realization that he is dealing with an absolute stranger. It is one thing to have a pleasant chat for 20 minutes, but it is another thing to actually sit down and do business. The man wants to know more about you, but is usually reluctant to ask, and takes the easiest way out, which is to decide not to make a decision. Your problem now is to create the confidence in yourself and your firm which will overcome his indecision.

Bring with you any or all of the following:

(a) Your firm's financial statement.
(b) Past newspaper advertisements placed by your firm.
(c) Any write-ups received by the firm in the Wall Street Journal.
(d) Any favorable publicity about yourself.

Best of all, if you can prevail on the Research Department to send a man with you, this will make an excellent impression!

You may not open the account on the call back, and you may have to make a second call back, but that should be the last one necessary to open the account.

Making the Cold Calls Into Lukewarm Calls

Cold calls can be made luke-warm with a preliminary mailing. To each of your cold call suspects, send a personal letter such as the following:

Dear Mr. Front:

Our representative, Mr. Dan Newton, will call on you Monday, the 5th of April, 3:45 P.M., to discuss a matter of interest to you. We thank you for your courtesy in seeing him.

Yours truly,

Halter, Granes & Co.

The letter will have to be signed by a partner or manager. Getting out two or three such letters a day presents no problem. The letter must be individually typed, however, and should be mailed with a stamp instead of being run through the mailing machine. This may sound like an idiosyncrasy, but it is not. It is the personal nature of the letter which will make it easier for you to see the man. That little stamp gives the added personal touch. Investing is a highly personal business. Next to the man's physician and accountant, you will know more about him than anyone else. In every way possible, you need to maintain the personal touch. Mail the letters out two days before your call. You will then be calling on him the day after he receives the letter. The letter tells nothing. It is only an attention-getting device, one which should arouse his curiosity.

Other attention-getting mailing pieces which can be used include your firm's Market Letter, or any of the literature listed in Chapter 16. Send the literature with a handwritten note on your personal memo pad, such as:

Dear Mr. Front:

This could be of interest to you. I'll be in your building on Tuesday and will take the liberty to stop by and discuss it with you.

Sincerely,

The lukewarm call needs a different technique than the cold call. Your first 30 seconds in the man's office will be the most critical. After all, you did send him a letter stating that you would discuss a matter of interest. He's going to want to know as soon as you come in just how interesting your discussion will be. Your opening sentences must grasp his imagination. What you say must fit the time at which you make the call. Some sample attention-graspers are:

"I came to see you because:

1. "With the Dow Jones at new highs, many investors have stocks which are still low."
2. "The recent dip in prices makes several situations attractive. Can I tell you about the three stocks we think are bargain-priced?"
3. "The general business situation is uncertain. We recommend two stocks which should not be held at this time. Can I tell you about them?"
4. "We are seeking new accounts in this area and want to tell about our up-to-the-minute recommendation for purchase. I have a copy with me. May I show if to you now?"

The chances are the suspect will see you. But again, he is far from prepared to do business with you. Inasmuch as you have made a specific recommendation, he will make note of it and wait to see if your suggestion rises in price. If it does, your chances of getting the account on a follow-up call are good. If it goes down, you can take the effort to explain why, but it is very unlikely that he will do business with you. This "wait and see" attitude is most prevalent among businessmen—they want to test you before they commit themselves.

And so, after you have made your cold call and presented your product, your success will probably depend upon the choice of investment. We are assuming here that in calling on businessmen, many of them are willing to assume risk and that you will be recommending aggressive-type securities. However, do not forget to ask the suspect if he buys speculations. He may wish investment grade issues, and you should also be prepared to recommend the better quality securities.

CHAPTER 15

KEEPING YOUR CUSTOMERS

AFTER A FEW MONTHS, YOU FIND YOURSELF feeling proud of the way your file of customer account cards is growing. But, as you relax later that day, the thought occurs to you that the acquiring of each account was the result of considerable effort and you would not like to lose any of your accounts. You must now allot more time to customer relations.

Record-Keeping Keeps Accounts

The first step in customer relations is to make sure that you maintain a precise record of each account's purchases and sales. The next step is to maintain contact no matter whether the account is active or inactive. Since you will be speaking to active accounts frequently, the problem is to maintain relations with the dormant account. The simplest method is keeping the account on a mailing list, maintained by your firm or yourself. You can see to it that each account receives the firm's Market Letter when issued. Do not, however, expect your accounts to understand the significance of what they are reading. Where you believe a recommended issue suits the needs of one of your accounts, follow the mailing with a phone call, and personally recommend it to the customer. Accounts are like wives—they don't like to be taken for granted. They still expect attention after the "marriage." They may not buy each time you call, but when they do decide to buy it will be from you and not from someone else. If you come across a news item about any of your client's holdings, either call the client to tell him about it, or clip it out and mail it to him. If you have several clients interested, in this age of duplicating machines, it is not difficult to send each a copy. Again, your contact will not lead directly to an order, but it serves notice on your clients that you are watching their holdings, and at the least will keep the customer for you.

Report the Bad News as Well as the Good News

You will, of course, call your more important clients immediately when any good news comes across the news ticker. Do the same if bad news comes across. Don't hesitate to call your clients if some news comes out which may depress their holdings. It is your job to advise them immediately and give them the opportunity to sell. You will not be held responsible for something which occurred over which you have no control, or which you could not foresee.

Also, call if any unusual activity shows up in someone's holdings. Your record of customers by name of security held will be invaluable at this time. You pull out the record for that security, on which is listed each customer's name, and call each one immediately. Your fast service will be appreciated. Not only will it help you keep the customer, but it may also lead to some immediate orders.

Accounts Like Small Attentions

Be prepared to do such unproductive things as advising customers when they received dividends and the amounts of same. Such information is usually desired prior to income tax time. You will also be asked to transfer securities from one name to another. Of course, your firm does the paper work, and neither you nor the firm receives anything for it, but it is a necessary function. When called upon to do these things, find out if any significant changes have taken place in the family. For instance, a new grandchild may lead to the opening of a Custodian account. A daughter's marriage should lead to your being introduced to the son-in-law; either he or members of his family may be investors. Again, use every opportunity to get prospects, and what better way than to use the "unproductive" functions you are called upon to perform?

Is the Account Worth the Effort?

Always weigh the amount of service required by the account against the business received. Where service outweighs business, cut down on service, and if the account *demands* the service, drop the account. Your time is too valuable to be used unproductively.

Some accounts will have to be entertained to be kept. Where you have a substantial account, do not hesitate to invest in certain amounts of entertainment. You will build a strong personal relationship, and the account will stay with you because of that relationship. However, don't be cajoled into doing this unless the account really merits the extra attention. The attitude of such persons is that they are providing you with commissions and should be repaid in the form of entertainment. Your attitude is that those commissions were honestly earned through hard work and service, and there is no reason to repay the customer for your efforts in his behalf. The commissions in the securities business are too small to be dissipated in unnecessary extravagances. Some customers, especially in walk-in offices, will make a point of coming to your desk at lunch time and having you buy their lunch. This is alright on occasion, but some will make a daily habit of doing this. At your discretion, if the customer merits the expense, do so; but if he does not, arrange to have appointments at that time. He'll stop.

If your home or apartment lends itself to entertainment, you might invite a few of your customers into your home. It is usually cheaper to do so than to go out to dinner, and you can fulfill your obligations in one night rather than in several nights.

Since entertainment is a legitimate tax-deductible expense, make sure you keep a record of all your expenses.

Be careful to follow the Exchange regulation on gift-giving. An unusual gift can be interpreted as a rebate on commissions, which, of course, is not allowed.

In general, your attitude towards entertainment and gifts should be that they are only an acknowledgement of a business relationship. You do not owe gifts and entertainment to your customers. It is merely a courtesy on your behalf. As a stockbroker, you are performing an important service for your accounts, and they *are* your accounts only because of your capabilities, and not because you pay them back in gifts and entertainment.

Think of this: When did your physician ever take you out to dinner? You go to him because you have confidence in him, and not because he buys your lunch.

Keep Up With Your Account's Personal Life

Although yours is a business relationship, maintain an interest in your account's personal affairs. As part of your record-keeping, you maintain personal data on each file card. When the customer calls you or you call him, keep the file card before you. Inquire about those little personal things which mean so much to each of us. Ask him about vacation plans; how his children are doing; his opinion about his industry; how his golf game is going. And do so with sincerity. Anyone who has entrusted their money to your supervision deserves your personal touch.

For gala occasions, such as a wedding, anniversary, bon-voyage party, etc., you can send something appropriate, and even a 25¢ greeting card may very often be sufficient. It is your thought which is important. If you send nothing, it will not be missed, because you, not being a member of the family or a close friend, are not *expected* to remember the occasion. But the fact that you *do* remember makes your card or gift that much more significant.

Remembering a customer's birthday can help cement your relations, and also help to get business directly. After acknowledging the birthday with a card, call him back in a week or two, and remind him that he is getting older and that he should strongly consider the profit-sharing retirement plan for his business, or that college plan for his children which he has been delaying.

Each birthday my insurance agent sends me a birthday card. As a fellow salesman, I asked him why. He told me that it was to impress me that I was growing older and consequently my insurance was becoming more valuable— the older you get, the more difficult and expensive it is to get insurance! Our customers also have to be reminded that as they grow older, their investments assume more and more importance, and that they should add as much as possible to their holdings during their productive years.

What to Do When His Stocks Go Down

The crisis in customer relations comes when the securities you have recommended go down. The first step in avoiding this crisis is to have made, at the beginning, a fair and honest presentation wherein this possibility was brought out. If you forewarn of this possibility, half your battle is won. When his securities do go down, or show signs of weakness, find out the reasons why and call the customer. *Do not wait until he calls you.* Psychologically, you will have the upper hand if you call him. Show him that you are not avoiding your responsibilities, but are willing to meet them head on. You may have a bad 15 minutes talking to the customer, but it is better than losing the account. Of course, you must present a logical reason as to why the decline occurred, and you must also recommend a course of action, which may be to hold, sell, or buy to average out the cost. In periods of severe decline, calling your customers is of paramount importance. At such time they will be most susceptible to the prospecting calls of other brokers, and if you don't talk to them, another broker will take away the account. (This should also be a hint to you to continue soliciting accounts during market declines. You may very well come across some other broker's accounts which he neglected to call, and you may appropriate the account for yourself.)

Don't Let the Mood of the Market Influence You

The tendency of many brokers is to let the swings of the market influence their personal moods, and in a downswing they let their emotions get depressed. They either refuse to talk to the customer with the excuse "What can I say?," or, if they do talk, do so with apologetic and mournful voices.

You must maintain your optimism at all times. No one invests for pessimistic reasons. The customer expects you to see better possibilities in the future, and wants you to point out why you expect things to get better. Anyone who looks back to the long record of the American economy sees an upward trend over the long term. Investors in American securities, whose securities are supervised and periodically reappraised, have done well. The uninformed speculator usually has suffered.

And so, in keeping customers, you have to re-evaluate each account's holdings periodically. Go over each account at least once a month. At this time your firm usually provides you with an end-of-month statement for each account. Where securities have been delivered, you will have the record in your book.

Look over each customer's list of securities and ask yourself if, in light of his objectives, his present holdings still are suitable. You may be reluctant to call and recommend changes because the choice was yours in the first place, and you will now have to explain why you changed your mind. Again, if the customer had been prepared properly during the interview and presentation phase, your job would be easier. He would know that no security is the ultimate answer to the problems of today, tomorrow, and yesterday. But, you must suggest replacements, or else the portfolio of securities may not perform well and you will lose the customer. Whether the customer holds one security or two dozen, you must recommend changes when conditions warrant a change. This of course means commissions to you, and should be done as a necessary service for which those commissions will be earned. The representative who recommends changes when unnecessary, or suggests changes too frequently, leaves himself open for a charge of "churning." For the customer's benefit and your own, make sure your reasons are valid.

One Customer Leads to Another

The satisfied customer is your best source of new customers. When you have established a sound relationship with your customer, ask him to refer people to you. Ask for the name of just one person you may contact, and ask for permission to use his name. After you have one name, then ask for another. Customers are reluctant to turn over their whole acquaintanceship to you, and it is easier to get the names one at a time.

There is a deep sense of personal gratification to be derived from this business. When your customers stay with you because of fair and equitable treatment, and call upon you for advice, you can take pride in knowing that you are doing a good job. You will then realize that you are not in this business just to make money, but also to make satisfied customers—the money will follow.

CHAPTER 16

THE SALES PROMOTION MATERIAL AVAILABLE TO YOU

AN ENORMOUS AMOUNT OF SALES AIDS ARE available to you at little or no cost. The New York Stock Exchange provides all of the material described below, and we have added our comments as to how to best use the material. The figures given are the price per unit:

> *Investor's Notebooks, 1 & 2.* To gain the interest of new investors. Can be mailed to prospects or given to cold call suspects. 5¢

> *Does it Make Sense for Me to Buy Stocks?* Use for new investors. It answers the basic questions about investing. 5¢

> *Investment Facts.* Use like *Investor's Notebooks.* It also contains a brief description of M.I.P. 4½¢

> *How to Get Help when You Invest.* A basic primer for new investors with built-in reply card. Excellent for a mailing campaign to get prospects. 5¢

Understanding Preferred Stocks and Bonds.   For those interested in senior securities.   9¢

The Language of Investing.   A glossary of investment terms. Give it as a souvenir to someone who has just opened an account with you.   5½¢

How to Understand Financial Statements.   Good for the more sophisticated investor. Use it to get interest or as part of a mail campaign to get prospects.   8¢

Understanding the New York Stock Exchange.   A basic primer on the workings of the Exchange. Distribute when giving talks to groups or as an educational piece for the less sophisticated investor. Expensive looking.

10¢

The Nation's Market Place.   A brief colorful description of the Exchange. Use it as a mailing piece to prospective clients to maintain interest.   2½¢

The Stop Order.   Explains what the "stop order" is, and should be used for investors whose knowledge of the market has to be expanded. There is a great deal of misconception among investors about the mechanics of the stop order.   9¢

The Exchange Magazine.   A very informative magazine issued each month with background stories on listed companies. Makes an excellent mailing piece to your present clients, who will remember you at least 12 times a year when they receive it.

Subscription price $2.00
for 12 issues

How to Invest on a Budget.   Both explain the story of M.I.P. For use with new investors and as a suggestion to old accounts to meet such future needs as retirement or college.   5¢

Envelope Enclosures. Easily understood explanations of many investment terms. To be used in mailings to customers and prospects.

> "What's the Financial Health of Your Stocks?"
> "Taking the Mystery Out of XD"
> "Donations of Securities May Offer You Significant Tax Savings"
> "The Systematic Way to Invest . . . M.I.P."
> "The Odd-Lot System"
> "Are Rights Worth Exercising?"
> "Dollar Cost Averaging"
> "Averages"
> "Ratios"   ¾¢

> *M.I.P. Self-Mailer.*   A three-way folding card which needs only to be addressed and mailed. Your addressing precludes having to fill in his name. He simply sends back the pre-addressed reply card. Excellent for mass mailings at low cost.   3¢

For talks before large groups, and as part of your program before clubs and societies, the following materials are available:

> *Single Date Speech Outlines.*   Six outlines for one-time talks for the various types of organizations you are likely to come before.

> *Investment Club Information Kit.*   A comprehensive package of materials for organizing and operating an investment club.

Several excellent motion pictures which can be used as the focus for an evening's talk, or discussion before groups, are:

> *What Makes Us Tick.*   A color cartoon explaining the workings of the Exchange.   12 minutes

Your Share in Tomorrow. The award-winning film on share ownership in America. 27 minutes

Working Dollars. The story of M.I.P. in a color cartoon. 13 minutes

The Lady and the Stock Exchange. Janet Blair and Eddie Bracken in a basic story for the new investor. 27½ minutes

All of the above may be borrowed without charge. The group should supply the projector, but if they do not, don't hesitate to arrange for one in order to give the presentation.

Not only has the Stock Exchange provided a tremendous amount of material, but the Mutual Funds also provide plenty of promotional matter. The list below is only a part of what is available, and although only three funds are selected as examples, they are chosen only for illustration and not as an endorsement of the individual fund.

Much of the mutual fund material requires an accompanying prospectus or a prior mailing of a prospectus. Be sure to comply with this regulation. You could mail a prospectus first and subsequently mail the sales pieces as a follow-up.

Vance Sanders & Co., distributors of the Massachusetts Trust Group of Mutual Funds, have the following brochures available:

The Richest Man in Babylon. A fable set in ancient Babylon which is timeless in its advice on gaining wealth. Can be used for all types of prospects, but is especially good for systematic plans. Brochure cost: none, in reasonable amounts

Many Far-Sighted People Invest in Growth Stocks. In clear, simple language, explains the risks and possible rewards of selecting growth stocks for one's investment program. Brochure cost: none, in reasonable amounts

Wellington Co., distributors for Wellington Fund and Windsor Fund, provide the following at no cost:

Three-Way Mailing Cards. Good for an inexpensive mail campaign to seek out prospects.

Savings & Loan Comparisons. For the new investor who has to decide between keeping surplus funds in the bank or investing same.

Starting Today to Enjoy Tomorrow. Shows the uses for a Mutual Fund investment plan in easy-to-understand terms for the unsophisticated investor.

Financial Planning Data Sheet. Provides you with a form to enter the prospect's financial situation properly for future analysis.

Profit-Sharing Retirement Kit. A complete set of forms and instructions for setting up a profit-sharing plan in the corporation—only the figures have to be filled in.

A Guide for Selling Mutual Funds. This pamphlet is an excellent sales primer for new representatives.

Putnam Fund Distributors include among their literature:

A Message to a Man Worth $100,000. A provocative piece for the large investor who tries to handle his own investments. Can also be sent to those who don't have that amount of money to illustrate how the smaller investor gets the same benefits as the large investor in Mutual Funds.

A Bird in the Hand.   Explains the why and wherefore of growth investing.

Suppose I Don't Live That Long.   The contractual plan with diminishing-term life insurance is explained.

Teach your Wife to be a Widow.   Reprint of this shocker which makes a man think about his financial health as well as his physical health. Use it on complacent and hard-to-move customers.

21 Ways to Save Taxes on Your Investments.   Helpful aid for any investor. Use it as a give-away piece for clients and prospects.

Discover the Fortune Hidden in Your Salary.   For the prospect who tells you he doesn't have any money. Shows him how a small fortune dribbles through his hands during his lifetime and how he can get to keep part of it himself.

3-Way Mailing Cards.   For the contractual plan with diminishing-term insurance; an inexpensive mail campaign piece.

Some Examples of How to Use Literature

After having selected the literature you wish to work with, order a supply and keep the material near you.

1. As you go through your calls, send out an appropriate piece after your conversation. If you just got through talking to a customer about the earnings of a company, and you had to explain the income statement, send him a copy of *How to Understand Financial Statements,* with a personal note; having spoken to a prospect who wants to

keep surplus funds in the bank, send a comparison of Mutual Funds and Savings and Loan deposits.

2. During quiet periods of the day, address three-way mailing cards and see to it that they get mailed out that day. Try to write a minimum of 50 pieces a day.

3. The brochure, *Message to a Man with $100,000,* can be used as a mailing piece (with prospectus) to be followed with a cold call. It makes for an excellent door-opener.

Prepare a canned opening talk such as in this illustration:

"Mr. Prospect, my name is ———— of ————— ———— & Co., a firm of investment brokers. Yesterday you received a *Message to a Man with $100,000.* Mr. Prospect, I don't know if you have $100,000, but wouldn't you like to know how a man with $100,000 should invest his money?" (Wait for the "yes" or "no" answer.) If the answer is "Yes," as it usually is, ask for an appointment. If the answer is "No," then say, "Mr. Prospect, although no one can guarantee the future, would you like to learn how others have acquired $100,000 in the past?" (Wait for the "yes" or "no" answer.) If the answer is "Yes," ask for an appointment. If the answer is "No," forget about the prospect.

4. Most any interesting piece of literature can become the focal point for a cold telephone campaign, with a little imagination and a lot of hard work. It is the most convenient way to go prospecting because you can do it right from your desk, and to the new man who has few customers, what else better do you have to do with your time?

A program of canvassing by telephone can be built around many of the brochures just listed. When making the calls, prepare a written presentation which you will read over the phone. The purpose of this is to keep you from making errors in speech, and by focusing your attention on the words before you, you will not have the time to worry about the man at the other end of the wire. You will work with greater relaxation.

5. Women represent over 50 percent of share owners. Call upon them with an idea which will appeal to them, using the pamphlet, *How to Invest on a Budget.*

For businessmen, try this approach:

"Mr. Prospect, my name is —————— of ——————
——————, a member firm of the New York Stock Exchange. I just sent you an article, *Teach Your Wife to Be a Widow,* and it was purposely sent because many businessmen spend so much time trying to make money that they haven't the time to put their financial house in order. We can assist you in keeping your finances in order. May I see you on Tuesday or Wednesday of next week?"

Do not give any further information on the phone and insist on a face-to-face appointment. When you come to the interview, be prepared to ask all the necessary questions so that you may make your analysis and presentation.

6. Using the brochure which describes the New York Stock Exchange movie, *The Lady and the Stock Exchange,* send copies to women's organizations and call with an offer to show the movie at their next meeting, along with a brief talk on investing.

Anything Can Happen—and Will

Again, don't be surprised at the responses you get. On a campaign to sell M.I.P., you may very well get trading accounts. On a campaign to the "well-to-do," you may get Mutual Fund plan accounts. Don't categorize any group you call upon, and do not try to predetermine the investment course of any individual. Only after you have asked the right questions and have received the right answers, can you know what the prospect will buy or sell.

All of the literature listed above, and the sample campaigns for their use, are primarily a means of prospecting. You are, so to speak, just going to get your foot in the door. Once past the first barrier, you still have to go through the sales process. The job of looking for prospects is only a small part of the bigger job of making sales, and should not be treated as an end in itself. You can be a good canvasser and a poor closer of business. Just as in golf, the player with the longest drives can miss the putts. If you are good in one facet and poor in another, you might consider working together with another man as a team. One will do the canvassing and the other will make the actual call in person. Two men working as a team can accomplish more than one individual, and although the idea has never been popular, it merits the serious attention of the man who has confidence in another's ability as well as in his own.

Keep abreast of the new literature which comes out, and use it in your work. Pieces of sales literature, are, like drops of rain, needed to cultivate clients.

CHAPTER 17

YOU HAVE FRIENDS STANDING BEHIND YOU

THE NEW YORK STOCK EXCHANGE, THE AMERI-
can, the N.A.S.D., and other exchanges are
looked upon by registered representatives as
regulatory agencies who see to it that each man
conforms to the strict rules and regulations of
the securities business. To some, the rules cause
discomfort, and to others, the regulations may
seem a necessary evil. But to registered representatives, the rules are the backbone of the
securities business.

There would probably be no public participation in the stock market without the self-
regulatory aspects of the Exchanges and the
N.A.S.D. The rules and regulations of Exchanges and the N.A.S.D. help create the confidence needed to bring customers into the
securities markets. Each registered representative, by adhering to the rules, makes his cus-

tomers feel secure in the knowledge that they are dealing with a firm of high integrity. The securities business is too sensitive not to be hurt by the slightest malpractice on the part of one of its participants. A wrong-doing by one hurts everyone.

For example, the New York Stock Exchange keeps a blanket bond over each firm and its personnel to protect customers against fraud. It must be a comfort for an investor to know that he cannot be defrauded if he deals with a member firm.

All the Exchanges and the N.A.S.D. set high standards of business ethics and integrity. In what other business are millions of dollars' worth of orders taken daily on a verbal basis? Each transaction is usually the result of a telephone conversation of which there is no written record. Thousands of individuals daily agree to buy and sell with just a telephone call. No written order or signature is required. Unless individuals knew that they were dealing with a businessman of integrity, these transactions could not exist. Customers know they will receive fair and equitable treatment, and they also know that, if left unsatisfied, they will have recourse to the regulatory agencies to settle their grievances.

By insisting on competent training for its representatives, the Exchanges and the N.A.S.D. provide that the man who services accounts will be prepared to do the best job possible. By its system of inspecting offices and the registered representatives in those offices, the Exchanges and the N.A.S.D. see to it that due diligence is maintained in the servicing of accounts.

Because of the above-mentioned practices, confidence in the investment community is at an all-time high, and by 1965, 20 million Americans had become shareholders because of this condition; your job of getting accounts has been made that much easier.

Your customers also have the protection of minimum commissions on listed securities as set by the Exchanges, and a spot review of commissions and mark-ups by the N.A.S.D.

Your Friend at 11 Wall Street

There is a great amount of advertising done by the New York Stock Exchange in national magazines. Of course, you have their advertisements in leading publications. Their theme is the importance of investigating before investing, and the investors' receiving of sound information from trained, knowledgeable representatives. The advertisements project an image of yourself as being well-trained, capable, competent, and pleased to be of service. They depict you as you must be to meet the exacting needs of the securities business.

The New York Stock Exchange creates and provides excellent sales literature and other promotional matter, some of which is listed in Chapter 16.

The Exchange sets standards of training and competence to assure that those who do become registered have a knowledge of the highly technical securities business— for the sake of those whom they will serve.

After training, the Exchange keeps watch on its representatives by sending investigating teams to their offices. They check over individual accounts and the representatives' records to see to it that the high standards of training are maintained in actual work. These visits are not meant as an Inquisition, but as a device to benefit all of us in the securities business by reminding us of our obligations to serve the public to the best of our abilities. Unless each of us maintains a sense of obligation, we will all lose prestige, public confidence, and business.

The New York Stock Exchange does a great deal of sales promotion work useful to the representative. For example, the sales letters issued by the Exchange are prepared and pretested so that you receive a sales tool ready to go to work for you. Should you wish to show a movie on investing to a group, the Exchange has several films for you to choose from. There are speech outlines for addressing clubs and societies. There are also advertising mats for "ads" in your local newspapers.

All of the promotional material is either free or available at nominal cost, and is of tremendous value to the man building a clientele.

If you are registered with the N.Y.S.E. as a representative, you also have certain privileges that go with your employment. Should you retire, M.I.P. and Mutual Fund plan commissions may be paid out to you during your retirement.

Should you come to grievance with your firm, the Exchange will act as arbitrator, upon request.

Your Friend at 888 17th St. N.W.

It is easy to understand how the securities business can attract the sharp operator looking for the easy dollar. The investigation of each new registrant prior to acceptance, and his supervision afterward, are, therefore, enormous but necessary tasks. The securities business is vital to our economy. Venture capital is always needed in a free enterprise system, and unless those who provide the capital are protected, there would be no corporate and municipal financing, and no free enterprise. If the swindler is allowed access to the securities business, he can undermine the foundations of our economy. Not only must we be aware of those who act out of greed, we must also be aware of those who act out of stupidity. The N.A.S.D. was created as a result of the Maloney Amendment to the Securities and Exchange Act of 1934. The function of the N.A.S.D. is to be watchful over its members in order that just and equitable practices are maintained. The N.A.S.D. members are subject to rigid inspection, and each time a violator of the rules is found out and expelled, the job of the honest members is made that much easier. The securities business cannot flourish without public confidence. One of the sources of that confidence is in knowing that in dealing with an N.A.S.D. member, they, the public, are being protected against fraud and deceit.

When a newspaper item mentions an expulsion from the N.A.S.D., it is not a black eye to the industry. It is living evidence of the N.A.S.D.'s desire, ability, and determination to keep the business clean. As for the registered representative, he has the satisfaction of knowing he is in a reputable business, and will be treated with the respect and courtesy due the sound businessman.

Your Friend at 61 Broadway

The Investment Company Institute has no regulatory powers. It is a trade association of the Mutual Funds. As such, its importance to you is in its promotional work. The

I.C.I. is fast embarking on a series of extensive advertising campaigns which will foster an understanding of Mutual Funds among the public. Initially, national magazines are being used. Reprints of the advertisements have been made available for the use of member firms, and are excellent mailing pieces. The national advertising will make your job of selling Mutual Funds easier.

The I.C.I. also publishes, each month, a record of Mutual Fund sales, both by cash and plans. You should avail yourself of copies, and match your sales efforts against the national figures. If sales are up all over the country and your personal business is not, then you had better determine what you are doing wrong.

Without the supervisory functions of the Exchanges and the N.A.S.D., and without the education program of the Exchange and the Investment Company Institute, your job would not be only difficult, but perhaps impossible.

The work that your three "friends" have done is not meant to stop at their doors. You, too, in your day-to-day business, need to educate the people you meet; and you, too, must continue to project the image set for you. Your public expects it, you need it, and your business demands it.

CHAPTER 18

LIVE UP TO YOUR IMAGE

IN ORDER TO BE EFFECTIVE WITH THE PUBLIC, you will have to live up to the image of the broker. People think of a broker as having a certain distinctive look and of being acute in his thinking. Our problem is to make the public recognize us as brokers not only by our inner abilities, but also by our outward appearance and manners. Let us then adopt those attitudes which will make us recognizable for what we are—participants in a strict and exacting business.

When you hear the word "stockbroker," what image comes to your mind? If you are like the public, it is that of a neatly and conservatively dressed man with a dignified, yet personable bearing. He exudes an air of confidence. He speaks in a distinct, yet modulated tone, and his voice carries with it the conviction that comes from a knowledge of his business. He is alert, has a firm grasp of current affairs, is conservative in outlook, but willing to assume sensible risks. His judgment is sound, and he weighs the relative merits of each market situation. He is a good mixer socially, but is never loud or ostentatious.

Everywhere you go—the theatre, the restaurant, a resort hotel, the gas station, the grocery—project the image of the stockbroker. Your clothes are always neat, clean, and in good taste. Your hair is cut often and well. The car you drive has a clean, polished appearance. No matter how hard you are striving for business, you do not show anxiety, or a need for business. You always appear as though you have enough business, but when the opportunity occurs, you will graciously accept just one more account.

By looking as a stockbroker should look, and by practicing behavior which one expects of a stockbroker, you will find yourself meeting people of means, who can give you sizeable accounts. A very successful man, now manager of a large office, learned the lesson of "appearance sake." T.W. came from a modest background. He had saved some money and had made a study of securities. His investments did well, and he decided to become a registered representative. He worked hard, but in his second year, he realized that he was obtaining only small accounts. In order to upgrade his business, he made an investment in himself. He had suits tailor-made, visited his barber each week, and spent each weekend at an expensive resort hotel where he met well-to-do people. His business increased tremendously, and he is an important producer today. Each time you are at a social function, you need not broadcast your business. Invariable someone will ask what you do for a living. Simply say "I'm a stockbroker"; the image this conjures up in the mind of the questioner will be sufficient. You will then be made the center of attention, because the stock market has become one of today's main topics. In keeping with your image, do not give out advice. A social function is hardly a place to discuss something as important as someone's securities. If someone wants your opinion, he should be willing to accept it in the privacy of office or home.

However, neither should you be stiff and formal to the point of appearing unapproachable. You might say "George, if your stocks are worrying you, don't you think we should discuss it in the privacy of your office instead of among all these people? The first day in the week I have some time, I'll call you. What's your number?" If you constantly talk, you will be like the girl who tells every fellow she meets she wants to get married. There is no surer way to chase customers away. But, by keeping about you the air of aloofness, as though you know much but aren't talking unless asked, your chances of getting inquiries are better. You can always get the conversation going, if you so desire, by asking the other party, first, what he does for a living. He is bound to ask you the same question in return.

On many occasions you may know beforehand whom you are going to meet at a social function. If, for instance, you know that a successful appliance distributor will be at the affair, be sure to study the latest trends and developments in the appliance business. When you meet this man, you will astonish him with your knowledge. He may consider you to be so astute a broker as to handle his account!

Oscar Wilde once said, "Nature follows Art." If you adopt the "art" of being a stockbroker, you will naturally have the broker's look about you. You do not need to go to great expense to accomplish what T.W. did. Judicious shopping for clothing will get you the suits you need at moderate prices, and you can meet well-to-do people through charitable work or political clubs.

Don't hesitate to take a possible client out to lunch. Remember, it is a tax-deductible item, and the man who accepts your lunch usually feels a sense of obligation. In keeping with your image, have your luncheon appointments in the same restaurant so that the owner or host knows you by name. Your guest will appreciate the fact that you are known.

You may wish to entertain in your home. It need not be pretentious. The success of entertaining is not the surroundings, it is the graciousness of the host. For a small sum, you can hire someone to serve, giving your wife and yourself every opportunity to mingle with the guests. It is wise to let your wife know why you invited certain people so that she will be able to assist you by providing you with the opportunity to speak with them. Many registered representatives use home entertainment effectively.

R.F. and his wife both worked—he as a registered representative, she as a teacher. They had many friends and acquaintances. In order to familiarize them with R.F.'s new position, they ran several parties at their apartment. They had not even completed furnishing as yet. Mrs. F. was a good cook and someone was hired to serve. R.F. is making rapid advances; his production increases each month. Their friends, mostly from college, look upon him as a stockbroker, and as their incomes increase, they turn to him for investment advice.

Look, speak, and act the stockbroker! Your profession demands it; your clients expect it; your income can depend on it. But to do so, you must develop your skills.

The stakes are high. The payoff can range from earning a good livelihood to being a failure. Which shall it be? Would you consider going into a boxing match without first training yourself to punch, duck, and counterpunch? Would you enter a swimming race without devoting hours of practice in order to develop a smooth stroke and kick? Did Sandy Koufax and Mickey Mantle come out of nowhere? Or was it a combination of ability and constant practice to develop skills which made these men outstanding?

You, too, must develop your skills in order to convert your abilities into dollars. Since most of your time will be spent on the telephone, the first skill to develop is the use of the phone. Hold the telephone mouthpiece close to your mouth and talk directly into it. Look at yourself in the mirror and see if you hold the phone correctly. If you do not keep your mouth in a direct line and close to the mouthpiece, the other party will have difficulty hearing you. Also, if you do not talk into the mouthpiece, your voice will carry across the office and help make it into a noisy place to work. Don't talk too loudly. It is better to be too soft than too loud. A soft voice is pleasant to the ear and gets more attention from the listener than the loud voice. Practice talking softly until it becomes habitual. In speaking, do not use monotones. If an orchestra played one note all the time, no one would listen. If they vary their tones and rhythms, however, the musical composition becomes more interesting. If they played very fast and very loud, they would drive the audience away. You, too, must raise and lower your voice as you speak. This change of pitch is most important in the securities business. You are selling an *intangible*. Everything you can do to lend color and concreteness to your presentation is of great help. People can't see, touch, smell, hear, or taste your product. You must describe it in tangible terms. The words you select must be carefully considered. Your voice should heighten the meaning of your words. The way you say a simple statement of fact can help make or lose a customer. Let us take this sample sentence:

> This company is expected to earn $3.50 a share this year as against $2.50 last year, and in our estimation, the current price does not reflect the anticipated earnings.

Here is a sentence which is well within the rules and regulations. You can speak it out in a monotone and make it sound as dull as it reads, or you can charge it with excitement—for it is a piece of exciting news—by changing the inflections of your voice. Now read the following sentence out loud and make it sound interesting:

> This company is expected to earn $3.50 a share this year as against $2.50 last year (I repeat: $3.50 against $2.50), and in our estimation, the current price does not reflect the anticipated earnings!

There are many sentences which you will repeat day after day. Practice them to make them sound interesting and alive. Let your wife or girl friend listen to you. If you have a tape recorder, practice the sentences on it. Here are some of the sentences you will use every day—make them sound vibrant!

> Good morning, Mr. Customer. Your Baxter Company just reported an increase in earnings—up 35¢ from last year. Isn't that great news?
>
> Hello, Mrs. Brown, I'm glad you called. By the way, Telephone Co. just sold at 72. What can I do for you?
>
> Mr. Fort, the outlook on Gammag Co. has changed. We've just revised our estimated earnings downward and suggest that you sell.
>
> Mr. Hacker, I don't believe a man in your position should buy Syntex. It's too risky. You should consider a utility with further growth prospects.
>
> Mr. Gove, this is Lou Bender. At 1:00 the averages are down 2 .29. Volume is moderate, steels and oils are weakest. Your stocks are down slightly. R.C.A. off ¼, Central off ¼, and Dow off ⅛. Is there anything I can do for you today? Thank you. I'll call you tomorrow.
>
> Mr. Hart, we've been doing business together now for three months and I presume that you are satisfied. Am I right? Mr. Hart, I'd appreciate a small favor from you. Can you give me the name of just one person who can use my services?

If necessary, take a public-speaking course. G.B., now a partner in a member firm, did:

G.B. entered the securities business after leaving accounting. He had never been in sales before. His sister was a speech teacher. He realized the importance of adopting proper speech techniques, and let his sister train him. He became an outstanding representative. The same intelligence which showed him the need for proper speech training helped him in solving the other problems which confronted him as a representative. In a few years, he was a partner in a member firm.

Stock brokerage is a glamor business in the eyes of the public, akin to advertising and motion pictures.

To the public, your business seems to be one of constant excitement. You are on Wall Street, the financial center of the world. In the mind of the public you live in a world that is fast, profitable, and knowledgeable. People think that in your world life is a swiftly-moving panorama, as it is shown in newspaper headlines—*Stocks Rise, Drug Stock Raises Dividend, I.B.M. Jumps 10 Points, Dupont Volume Leader, Pennsy Talks Merger,* and so on.

Your customers believe you live in a fast-paced world, and when they talk to you on the phone, they expect excitement in your voice. You could have spent the dreariest day—with a heavy downpour outside, the market piddling along at a 3 million-share volume, no change in prices, and not an order entered all day—but when you pick up that phone, your voice must reflect only vitality and energy.

Have you ever noticed how one store will always be full, while the same type of store across the street will be empty? Have you noticed how people prefer to go into the place that's busy rather than the place that is quiet? "Let's go in here," they say, "there are more people."

People want to do business in a place that bustles with activity. Just as they want to do business in a crowded store, they want to do business with a busy broker. They don't want to hear a dull, flat voice relate a series of facts and figures. They don't want an apathetic tone which makes everything said sound drab and boring. You are not announcing the arrival of a train when you give someone stock prices. You are talking to him about his money. He is vitally interested in his money. Your voice must reflect that interest.

Neither do they want to do business with a man who spends all day talking to them on the phone. The customer soon begins to wonder if he has any other customers.

Together with using your voice flexibly, your choice of words is important. You must be aware of semantics. The word which means one thing to you may have another meaning to someone else. There are words in the securities business which should not be used at all, because they carry connotations of the time when the business was unregulated and without ethics. Remove from your vocabulary such words and phrases as: *manipulate, manipulator, play the market, crash, inside tip, tout, sure thing, the insiders, dump stock,* and *gamble.*

Use "your securities" instead of "your stocks." The word *security* comes from the word *secure,* and is a better choice than the word *stock,* which, to many, connotes great risk. Use the word *speculate* with those who are in business and are used to and prepared to take chances—otherwise use the word *invest.*

Since you must do an enormous amount of reading, you should consider a speed-reading course. There are many such courses given at local colleges, and they are well worth the effort.

One excellent way to make contacts is through public

speaking. Investing is always a subject of interest, and if you make yourself into an interesting speaker, you can address many groups and develop many accounts. Do not take speaking engagements until you have taken some preparatory course in public speaking. The course can also be of importance in your day-to-day business.

There are many "myths" associated with the securities business. You will hear of a mythical "they," who push up stocks or push them down; of syndicates rigging the market; of insiders who know just what is going on and who take advantage of this fact. Invariably, these stories come from those who are active in the market, and who, despite the telling of such myths, continue to invest. One would expect that under such adverse circumstances they would not invest, but if one analyzes these myths, one can conclude that, like all myths, they are created to explain a phenomenon which the believer in the myth cannot understand. Thus, the ancient Greeks had their myths to explain the phenomena they did not understand, as do all unscientific people. The trader who expresses a belief in the Wall Street myths is only showing that he does not understand the stock market and uses the myths to hide his ignorance.

Most people have misconceptions about investing. Even owners of securities have many false notions about the securities business. Wherever you come across such notions, correct the individual. You will find people who believe that the Exchange buys and sells securities. You will find people who believe that each time they buy a stock, they are buying the broker's personal shares. You will find people who, if they lose money, believe it went to the broker. There are also those who believe you have secret information available only to those on the "inside," and that you can manipulate prices to your advantage. You will have to do your best to correct these false ideas, for the good of yourself and the entire investing community.

Another important skill is choosing words that will make your product understandable to the layman. Talk to people in language and in concepts they understand. The proper choice of words, or a picture drawn in words, can make *real* to someone the intangible you are trying to sell. If you are recommending a food chain, after you have related such dry statistics as price earnings, etc., say: "I'm sure there's an Apex Food Store near you. Ask your wife, she'll tell you how busy they are!"

If you are recommending an auto stock, "How many of your neighbors and friends own Gimmet cars? Their sales are way ahead of last year's."

If it's a paper stock: "How much more paper are you buying for your office this year than you did last year?"

If it's a Mutual Fund: "They diversify, which means they put your eggs in a lot of baskets."

Instead of saying, "Sales are up 10 per cent," say, "They are selling 110 units this year, while they only sold 100 last year."

"Of course we like the steel stocks. What's holding up the house you live in? What is your car made of?"

"I'll tell you why we think Electric Power is sound. Do you ever fail to pay your light bill? Of course not, and neither will any of their customers. In fact, they're using *more!* They are serving 30,000 new homes as of this year!"

Each time you make a presentation, think of the analogies which will make the stock seem real—something a person can see and feel. Here's an excellent way to show the effects of inflation:

D.W. wished to illustrate to a prospect the meaning of inflation. He enclosed a nickel in an envelope with a short note which said: "When you were a kid this bought an ice-cream cone, a hot dog, and a subway ride. It doesn't any more. That's inflation."

The most important skill to develop is effective speech. If need be, take a speech course at a college. The Dale Carnegie courses are also excellent for both speech and poise, and for the creation of self-confidence in dealing with others. The "Speak-Well–Sell-Well" course is also excellent.

Remember, you have it within yourself to become what you wish to become. The effort will be well worth it.